Coming to Terms with Divorce

*A Guided Support Program for
Primary Grades*

Workbook

by
Mary Ann Kuhn

A licensed school counselor and divorce recovery specialist, Mary Ann Kuhn is also an experienced teacher at the elementary grade level. She earned her M.A. in counseling at St. John College, Cleveland, and M.A. in family development at the University of Akron, Ohio.

Cover and Illustrations: Robin Smith

Copyright © 1992 The Center for Learning.
Manufactured in the United States of America.

ISBN 1-56077-146-1

Contents

Chapter 1 The Effects of Divorce 1

Chapter 2 My Journey through Loss 13

Chapter 3 My Feelings about Divorce 25

Chapter 4 My Feelings about Myself 37

Chapter 5 Words I Need to Know 47

Chapter 6 My Special Family 53

Chapter 7 Divorce and the School 63

Chapter 8 Little Tugs-of-War Inside Me 77

Chapter 9 Starting Over Again 87

Chapter 1
The Effects of Divorce

Something to Think about Before and After the Course

Directions: Take a red marker and circle the number that best describes your answer to each question. When you are finished with this book, return to this page and circle your answers to the questions with a blue marker. You will then be able to see how much you learned about these ten questions.

		No	Not Really	Kind Of	Yes
1.	Do you feel that you understand what divorce is?	1	2	3	4
2.	Do you think that you understand what your mom and dad have gone through?	1	2	3	4
3.	Do you feel that your mom and dad understand what you are going through?	1	2	3	4
4.	Do you feel that you are partly to blame for their divorce?	1	2	3	4
5.	Do you have someone to talk with about your parents' divorce?	1	2	3	4
6.	Do you wish that you had someone else to talk with about your parents' divorce?	1	2	3	4
7.	Do you know who to turn to for help when you have a big problem?	1	2	3	4
8.	Do you feel good about yourself right now?	1	2	3	4
9.	Do you have the feeling that you are the only child going through the kind of divorce problems that you have?	1	2	3	4
10.	Do you think that you will ever be happy again?	1	2	3	4

Some Important Things to Know about Divorce

Sometimes things happen to us that seem to turn our lives *upside-down* and *inside-out*. Can you remember ever having that feeling?

How about this example? There was a time when you might have lived with Mom and Dad and maybe even some brothers or sisters. Life seemed pretty great even though there might have been some unhappy times due to problems or fights or things like that. Then one day Mom and Dad told you they just could not live together anymore. WOW! What were they trying to say?

Those words were the way your parents were trying to begin to tell you that they were going to separate and maybe even get a divorce.

Separation means that Mom and Dad decide to live apart from each other. Some dads move across the country while some move to a little room in the basement. Mom might move three blocks away or to the next state. One parent stays with you while another parent moves. Where did your mom or dad move?

_____

Divorce often comes a year or so after the separation. This happens when Mom, Dad, and their lawyers go to the courtroom to see the judge. After hearing from the lawyers all the reasons why Mom and Dad cannot live together anymore, the judge decides that the marriage has come to an end.

So, divorce is when the court says the marriage is over. The changes that began during the separation happen more and more now. Things you used to do one way you might do a different way now. It does not mean, however, that all the old ways were good and all the new ways are bad.

Let's think about this, then add your ideas to the lists below.

Put a smiling ☺ face next to the things that make you happy, and put a frowning face ☹ next to the things that make you sad.

Things that happened before the separation/divorce.

We lived in one house.

There was fighting lots of times.

We went on vacations together.

_____

_____

_____

Things that happened after the separation/divorce.

We live in two places.

There is a lot less fighting.

I go one place with Dad and another place with Mom.

_____

_____

_____

Does Someone Know How I Feel?

It is important to say how you feel about divorce and the changes in your life. More than likely, you will see a change in the way you feel and act before and after the divorce.

Draw the face that best tells the way you felt before and after the divorce. Then, think of some words that describe these feelings and write them on the lines.

Before the divorce I felt
1. _____
2. _____

Before the divorce I felt
1. _____
2. _____

After the divorce I felt
1. _____
2. _____

After the divorce I felt
1. _____
2. _____

What Do I Do with All These Feelings?

Share the drawings on your faces and compare the different feelings. Why were some children sad before the divorce while others were sad after the divorce? It does not matter how you feel, but it does matter what you do with your feelings. Keeping them locked inside can cause you lots of pain.

Here are some ideas of what to do with your feelings. <u>Underline</u> in color the ones that you would like to do:

1. Talk with Mom.

2. Talk with Dad.

3. Talk with Grandma, Grandpa, or a favorite relative.

4. Talk with a friend who cares about you.

5. Tell someone at school who can help you, like a teacher or a counselor.

6. Do something that makes you feel better:

    play sports

    ride a bike

    play with a favorite toy

Now, add your own ideas on what to do when you feel very upset.

_____

_____

_____

_____

Hearing the News

Sometimes boys and girls have had some hints that Mom and Dad might be getting a divorce. Did you ever see any of these things happen? Check ✓ the ones that fit your Mom and Dad:

- ❑ Mom and Dad fought and yelled a lot.
- ❑ Mom and Dad never talked to each other.
- ❑ Mom and Dad never did fun things together.
- ❑ Mom or Dad were away from home a lot.

Now add some ideas of your own that let you know Mom and Dad were not as happy as they used to be:

_____

_____

_____

_____

No matter what you might have seen or thought, it is always hard hearing the news about divorce. It is even harder on the children who were never told anything until after Mom or Dad moved away. Parents do not like telling their children about the divorce, and kids do not want to hear anything about it. This makes it really hard for both the parents and the children.

How did you act when you were told about Mom and Dad's divorce? <u>Underline</u> the answers that show how you acted:

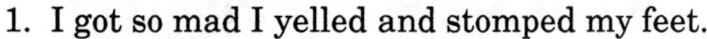

1. I got so mad I yelled and stomped my feet.

2. I felt so sad I cried and cried.

3. I sat and stared, not saying a word.

4. I tried to help a brother or sister.

5. I tried to talk Mom and Dad out of the whole idea.

6. I left the room.

Even though the day you heard the news was not one of your better days, the important thing is **you got through it!**

This is why this little book has been written . . . to show you that you can

    live through a hard time,

        get help from people who love you,

            learn how to hurt less and less,

                begin to make a happy life for yourself!!!

What Part of My Life Has Changed A Lot Since the Divorce?

Some adults are so upset themselves by the divorce that for awhile they cannot even think about what their children might be worrying about. Sometimes they simply do not know how to get their children to talk about their worries.

Look at the picture below. Let your teacher go around the wheel and explain some of the things that do worry children. Then, color the spokes on the wheel that bother you and that you would like to talk about sometime in the class.

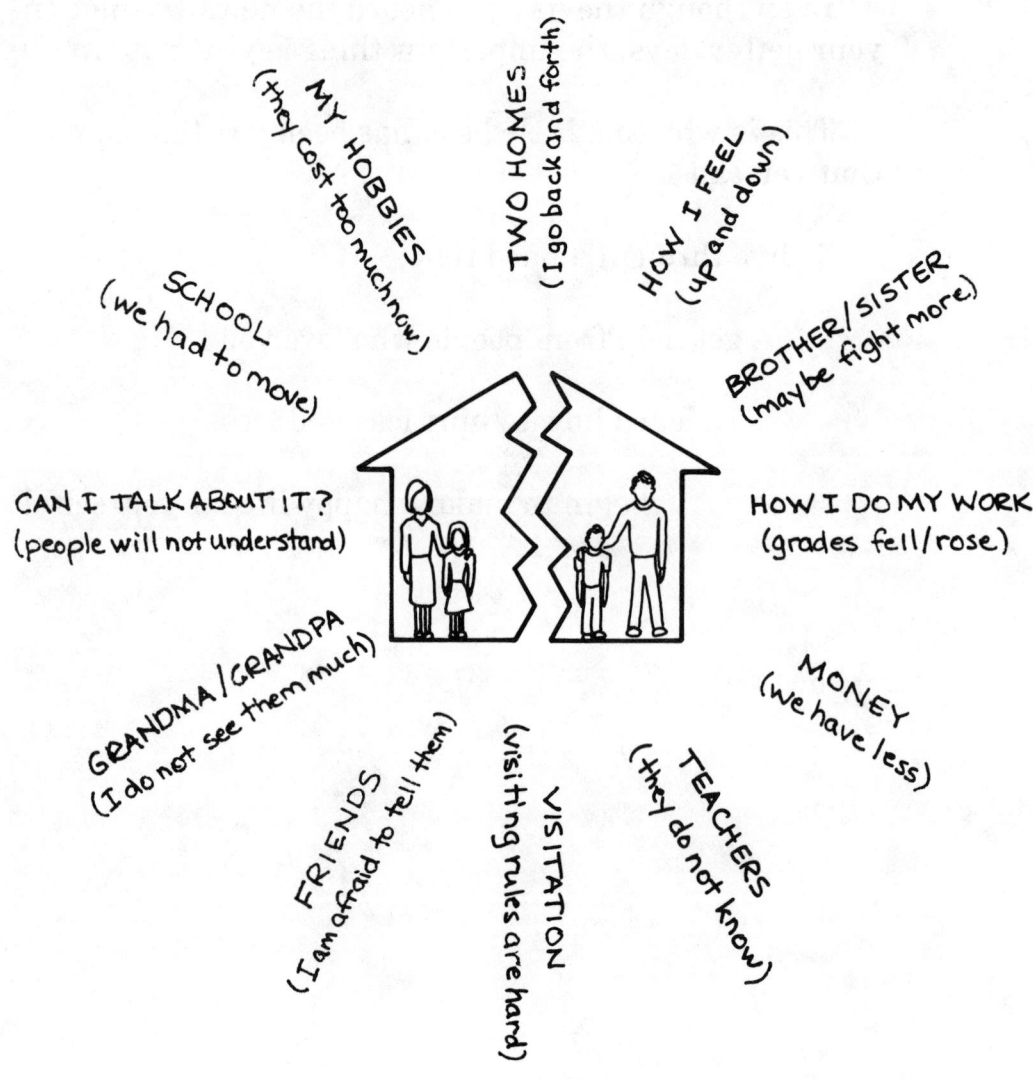

My Family Problems

One of the best ways to start feeling better when things go wrong for you is to know just what is making you feel so bad. Worrying about lots of things all at once makes you feel worse. Looking at one or two problems and learning how to solve these problems is a good way to start feeling better.

Here is a little exercise to help you explore just what might be a worry to you.

1. Answer the questions with the help of your teacher.

2. Color the balloons that best describe your biggest problems.

3. Write in the empty balloons any problems that better describe your family.

My family problem is _____

How does this problem bother me? _____

Who do I talk with about this problem? _____

What can I do to help myself feel better about the problem? _____

What could someone else do to help me with my problem? _____

Chapter 2
My Journey through Loss

What Is Happening to Me?

Before you can begin to understand what goes on inside you after Mom and Dad separate or divorce, you need to learn the meaning of two words.

Loss is the first word. Loss is the feeling that comes from being without something that you once had. Loss is a part of life. Nature teaches it to us every day:

Spring brings beautiful flowers.

Summer gives us bigger flowers.

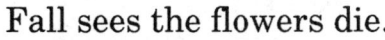

Fall sees the flowers die.

Winter lets the seeds prepare to grow underground.

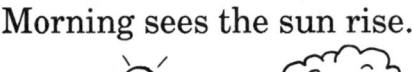

Morning sees the sun rise.

Noon brings much light.

Night brings darkness.

Crisis is the second word. A crisis is a very big problem that you often cannot solve yourself. Divorce is a crisis. When divorce happens in a family, children need caring people to help them understand what they are feeling.

This chapter will do just that . . .
    help you understand what is happening to you.

# Learning about Our Losses

Every little boy and girl, every mom and dad have many losses happen to them over and over in life. Knowing that losses happen is only part of the story. The harder part is asking **"How do you feel after your loss?"**

To help you answer this question, take a look at the following word.

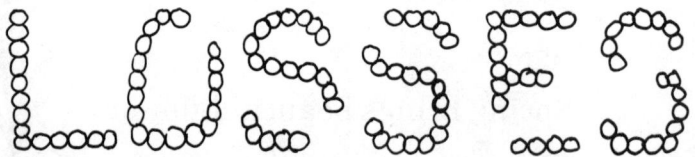

What do you see?
The word is not right, it is missing parts.

How does this make you feel?
You might not like the way the word looks. You want to make the word look right again.

We usually have these same feelings inside us when we go through losses.

Sometimes our losses are little and no one pays much attention to them.

But, they still bother us.

We feel bad,
and we want to make things better.

Other times in life we suffer very big losses.

After experiencing a very big loss,

We hurt inside,
We feel very alone,
We might be so sad we do not know what to do,
We want to make things the way they used to be.

 # Have Any of These Losses Ever Happened to You?

Study this page. It is divided into three parts; little losses, bigger losses, and very big losses. Underline the losses that you have had in your life.

Little Losses

My favorite toy was lost.

I lost my best sweater.

I got a low grade on a test.

I lost my lunch ticket.

Our family picnic was rained out.

I missed the school bus.

I forgot my homework.

I lost my recess.

Bigger Losses

I changed schools.

I lost a friend.

My pet died.

The other kids ignored me.

I got called names like "dummy" and "fool."

I'm not a cute little baby anymore.

Our new car was hit in the parking lot.

Very Big Losses

My mom and dad separated.

My mom and dad divorced.

One of my parents died.

A brother (or sister) of mine died.

Dad lost his job.

Our family moved.

Review: There are important lessons to learn from all of this.

☆ 1. Loss is a part of living.

☆ 2. Everyone has losses.

☆ 3. If you have gone through a loss, it does not mean that you are a bad person or that you deserved it.

☆ 4. You do not stay sad forever.

☆ 5. You can get over a loss and feel better as time goes on.

In this book we are choosing two of the "Very Big Losses" to learn about: *Separation* and *Divorce*. You will learn more about why you feel the way you do for months and years after Mom and Dad leave each other. This leads us to the next part of the "Loss Journey."

YOU CAN GET OVER A LOSS!

! What Is This "Loss Trip" All About?

After any big problem like separation and divorce, a person starts on a journey that travels inside the mind and heart. Everyone, both young and old, goes on their own little trip—each meeting ups and downs along the way.

Do you ever remember going on a trip with your mom or dad when something went wrong? Let's say that all the cars had to go very slowly on the turnpike because of road repair. You are both on the same trip, but you might have different feelings about the same event:

Dad (or mom) is very mad and shouts because this delay will make the trip last an extra two hours.

You are very sad and cry because you want to be in the pool at the motel.

Look carefully at the trip people take after the divorce. There are several important things to remember:

☆ 1. Everyone must make this "mountain climbing" trip after the divorce.

☆ 2. You should look for people and things to help you along the way.

☆ 3. Remember, you and your mom and dad are not always feeling the same way at the same time.

☆ 4. Even though it might not seem like it sometimes, you *will* reach the end of your journey.

☆ 5. Even though you will get through it, and new feelings will begin, your old feelings will continue on in your heart and mind, but to a lesser degree, for some time.

 # My Own Loss Journey

The Loss Journey
A Grief Diagram

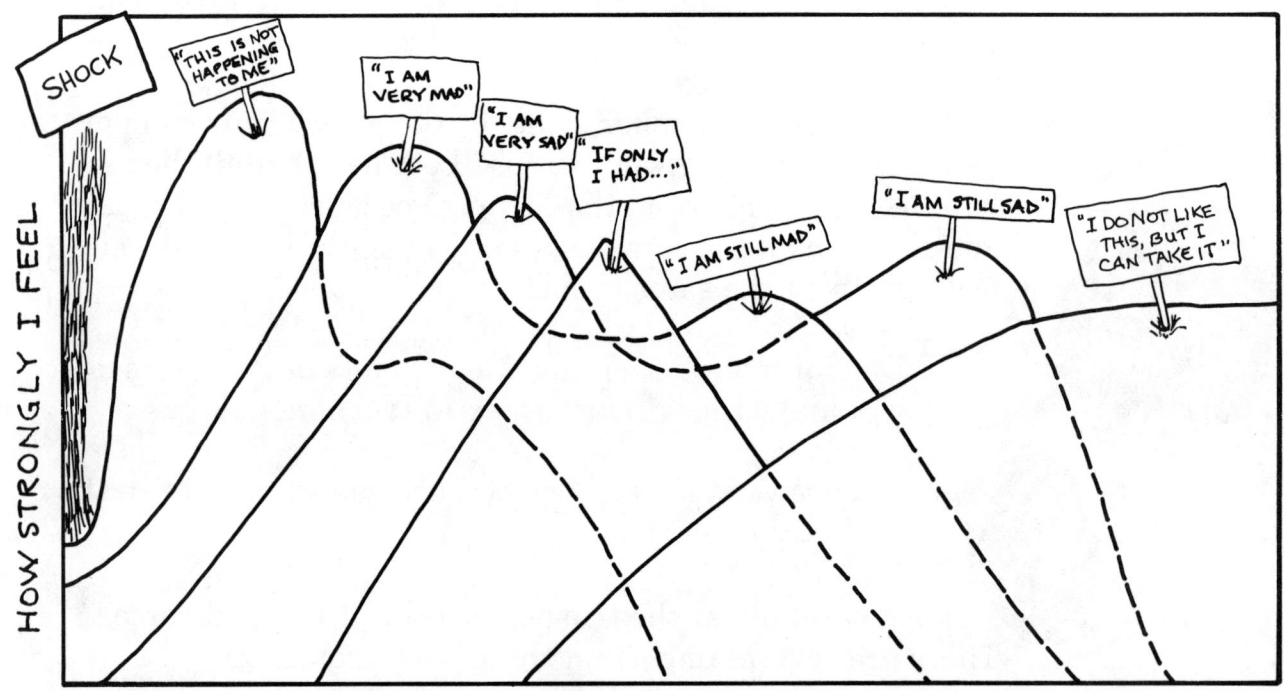

It is important to know what the mountains in the diagram mean. The following will explain the feelings you have along the way.

 **"Shock"** happens to you after you have learned some news that upsets you very much. For example, you are so stunned by the news that Mom and Dad are separating, you become numb for awhile.

 **"This is not happening to me"** takes place after the numbness goes away. It is an important stage because it gets you ready to face what is really happening. By creating a "dreamworld" where you say that everything is fine, you get yourself ready for the harder part of the journey.

You might find yourself saying

"Mom and Dad are really happy."

"Daddy just needs a vacation."

"No one in my family will ever get divorced."

At the same time you might be

fighting a lot

not playing with friends as much

"I am very mad." After a while you have some days where you begin to move out of your dreamworld. The first big feeling that takes over when your mom and dad are divorcing is *anger*. Feeling mad at Mom, Dad, yourself or the world is not bad or wrong—it is very normal. It is one way you ask people for help.

You might find yourself saying

"I hate Mom (or Dad)."

"Don't come near me."

At the same time you might

feel like you hate yourself

be blaming others for everything going wrong

The mad feeling is important for you to feel. This helps get the hostility out of your mind and heart. What you do to yourself and others when you are angry can cause you some trouble. Discuss with your class healthy ways of expressing anger. Here are some ideas to get you started:

Pound your pillow.

Hit a baseball or kick a football.

Ride your bike.

Walk or run.

"I am very sad" is another stage that is hard to climb over. This can begin to happen sometime after you know that

    Your dreamworld is over,

        Your "if onlys" did not work,

            You are tired of being mad.

Some children get sad on the inside because they lock their feelings up for a long time.

They find themselves saying:

    "I'm just a dummy."

    "No one on earth loves me."

Other children get sad on the outside by becoming mean to others.

They find themselves saying mean things such as

    "I'll pay you back."

    "Everything is your fault."

This stage can be a very lonely time with lots of tears and sad feelings. Some children act like babies at this point. Some choose to stay away from their friends and family. Feeling sad is OK, but you must let some people know how you feel so that they can love and support you. Who might you share your sadness with?

"If only I had . . ." After you get mad at lots of people for so long, you will stop being mad long enough to find yourself saying

    "If only I had been good, Dad wouldn't have left."

    "If only I had kept my room clean like Mom wanted, she would never have moved out."

This stage does not last long. It is your way of wishing that if you changed something about the way you acted it would make Mom and Dad change their minds—and you would make everything better again. This is *not true!* You did not cause the divorce and you cannot end the divorce.

STAGE 6: I DO NOT LIKE THIS, BUT I CAN TAKE IT

"I don't like it, but I can take it" is the last mountain that needs climbing. You know you have reached this point when you accept the way your family lives. You might not like Mom and Dad being divorced, but you face each day without being very sad or mad. In fact, you can be very happy and have a wonderful life.

You might find yourself saying

"This has been really hard, but we are doing pretty well."

"I can make it just fine."

You know you have reached this stage when you enjoy loving and trusting your family and friends again.

Now that you have learned what this journey is about, look again at "The Loss Journey—A Grief Diagram." *Color* the place on the journey where you think you are right now.

Remember

☆ This trip takes a long time.

☆ You can move backward and forward as you travel.

☆ Even though you are through the worst of the madness or sadness, you will still have these feelings sometimes, but it will never be as bad as it was in the beginning.

Packing My Bag for the Trip

Pretend you could take a suitcase packed with things that could help you on your "loss journey." Pack these ideas in your suitcase by writing them on the different pictures. An example is already done for you.

Remember: You need love and support as you travel on this journey!!!

(On the t-shirt:) I NEED TO TALK TO SOMEONE WHO CAN HELP ME

Chapter 3
My Feelings about Divorce

What Are Feelings?

One thing that everyone on earth shares in common is *feelings*. No matter who they are or how old they are, people know what it is like to be happy or sad, strong or weak, bold or bashful.

What are these things called feelings? Why do you have them? Are they good for you or do they get you into trouble? What kind of feelings do you have about the divorce?

For this chapter, let's pretend you can put on an imaginary thinking cap, climb into your *feeling machine* and explore your world of feelings.

The first stop of your journey is at the *Feeling Information Center*. The experts here want you to know some important things about feelings.

☆ 1. Every human being has feelings. They are a very important part of you.

☆ 2. Feelings are a way you can share on the outside what is going on deep inside of you.

☆ 3. Feelings are good and can help you in many wonderful ways.

☆ 4. A feeling is bad only when you use it in a wrong or hurtful way toward yourself or someone else.

☆ 5. Because of your memory, you can feel something this week, seem to forget about it for a long time, and still have that feeling come back months or years later. It is almost like you can "re-feel" what happened in the past. For example, last Christmas Sue got a bike. She was so excited she thought she would explode with happiness. Now when she thinks about it, she still feels great, but her feelings are not as strong as they were last Christmas.

**The next stop on your feeling journey
is to learn how others know what you are feeling!**

Sometimes you do not want to tell other people how you are feeling about something, like how proud you are of your report card, or how sad you are over your parents' divorce. And yet, others can still have an idea of how you feel. How can this be?

There are three main ways people can know how you are feeling inside.

1. By what you say to them:

    "I'm so happy that you came to play with me."

    "I don't want to play that game anymore, it's dumb."

    "Stay away from me!"

2. By the way you say something to them:

    In a pleasant tone

    In a mean tone

    In a very kind and loving tone

3. By the way you act:

    The look on your face

    The way you move

    The things you do

Draw a line matching the feeling with its clues.

Love

1. You are biting your nails.
   Your forehead is wrinkled.
   You feel scared inside.

Fear

2. You have a pleasant expression on your face.
   You feel good about another person or thing.

Joy

3. Your face is all red.
   Your heart is pounding.
   You have a mean expression on your face.

Anger

4. You feel very shaky inside.
   Your heart is beating very quickly.
   You want to run away.

Nervousness

5. You have a big smile on your face.
   You are jumping up and down.
   You are clapping.

# Learning New Feeling Words

An important stop on your feeling trip is the one that explores new ways to express your feelings. Everyday you can feel many different ways. You can feel mad, sad, happy, or afraid. You might feel different degrees of those feelings at different times. For example, you may feel very mad, or just a little bit crabby.

Look at the *Mood Roller Coaster* that follows. Moods are a lot like roller coasters—sometimes they are up and sometimes down. Find the *car* that describes how you feel right now. Color it! Then, underline the word or phrase under the car that might tell even better how you really feel.

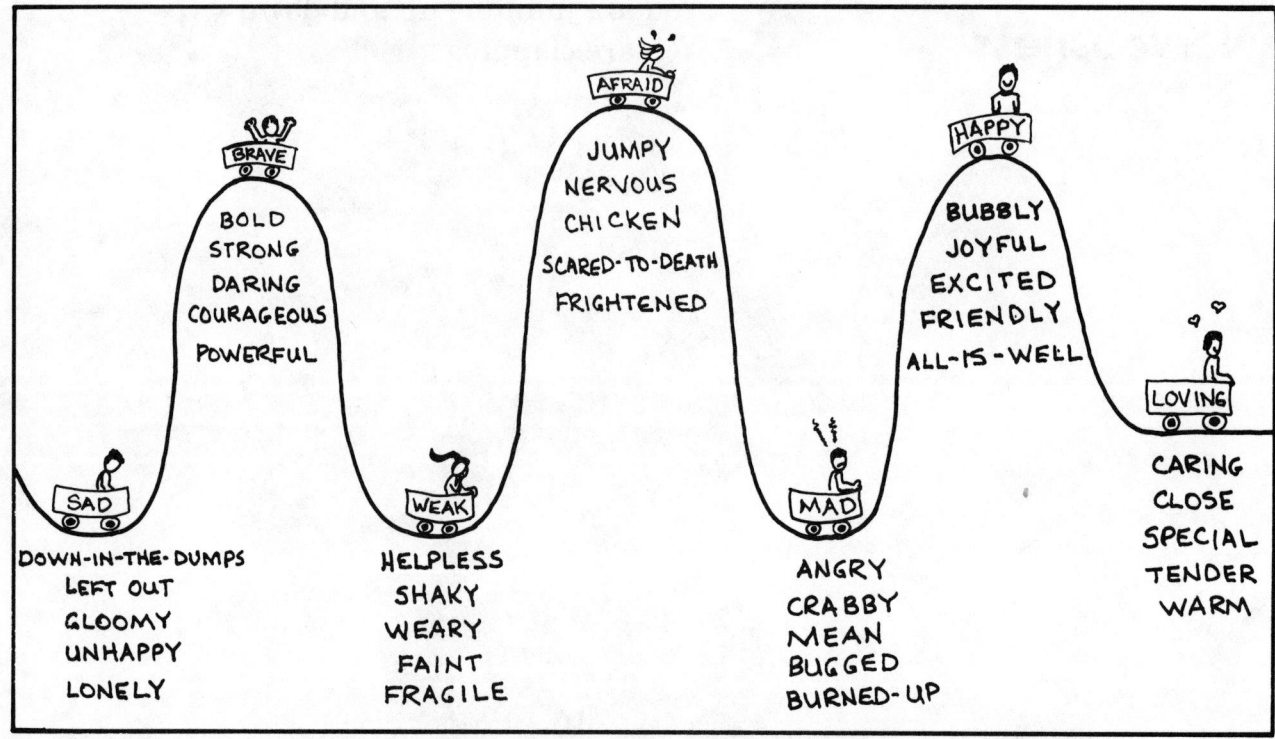

When parents get divorced, some children are happy the fighting is over, while others are sad that a parent is leaving. The following exercise will help you learn different ways children may react. Match the word in the first column with the roller coaster car above. Then find a feeling word below the car that fits in the blank spaces.

1. Mad   __ R __ B __ __

2. Sad   G __ __ O __ __

3. Afraid   __ __ __ P __

4. Loving   __ __ N __ __ R

5. Weak   __ H __ K __

6. Happy   __ U __ __ L Y

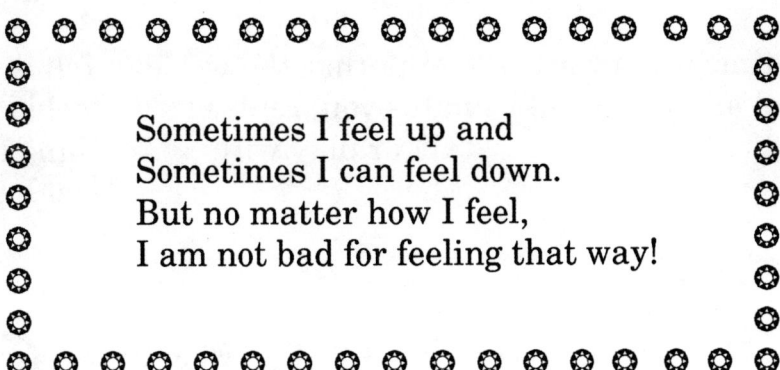

Sometimes I feel up and
Sometimes I can feel down.
But no matter how I feel,
I am not bad for feeling that way!

Handling Your Ups and Downs

Next on your feeling trip you will come to the land of the "ups and downs." In your world of feelings, it is very normal to feel "up" some days and "down" other days. You probably like your "up" days a lot more than your "down" ones. But, life brings you both, so the best thing to do is to learn how to handle those not-so-pleasant feelings.

Here are a few examples of what to do with some "down" feelings.

Feeling	What is it?	Poor ways to act	Good ways to act
Anger	A fit of bad temper	Hurt others, break toys, scream	Cry, hit a pillow, play hard (hit a baseball, ride your bicycle)
Loneliness	A time when you feel all by yourself	Think that the world hates you, refuse to talk or play with others	Tell someone that you feel lonely, do something that makes you feel happier

Now, discuss the next feeling with your class and then complete the chart on how to express your feelings.

| Sadness | To feel unhappy or gloomy | _____ | _____ |

One of the best things you can do for yourself is to learn healthy ways of expressing your feelings. To get started, think about the feeling of "loneliness" and draw a picture of what you could do to make yourself feel better on a lonely day. (You can do this on other days with any of your "down" feelings.)

My Feeling Shirt

Your feeling trip would not be complete without stopping to look at "The Feeling Shirt." You are growing up in a time when it seems like the whole world is wearing T-shirts with pictures and sayings on them. You do not have to go to a store and buy a shirt about divorce drawn by someone else. You have lived through it and have your own ideas.

Think of any picture that shows what you think about divorce, and draw it on the "Feeling Shirt." Then, think of a saying that goes with your picture. Put those words on the shirt also. Then, take time to share your pictures with the others in your class.

 # How I Feel about My Family

Before your "Feeling Trip" is over, it is good to realize how you are feeling right now about your parents' separation, divorce, or remarriage. A good way to do this is to look at a picture you make.

You are going to make two pictures appear on this paper, one of your family who lives with Mom, and one of your family who lives with Dad. Let's pretend that this is the year 3000 and we all live in space.

Start with the home (spaceship) you live in the most.

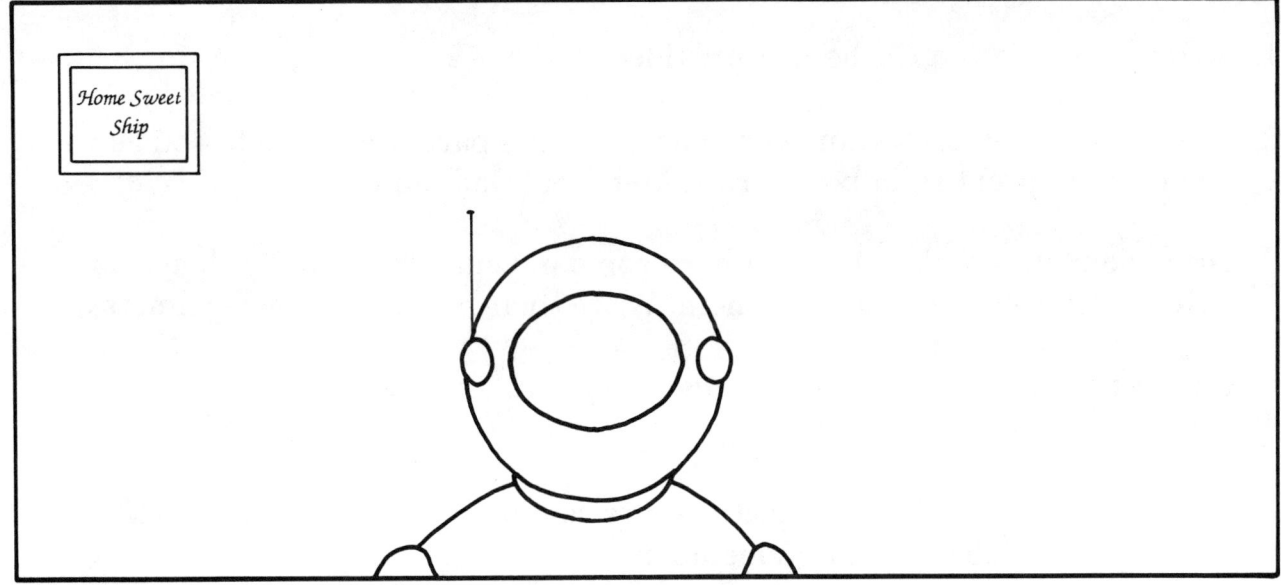

1. Write your name on the helmet already drawn for you.

2. Next, draw another helmet representing the parent who lives in this house and place it as close to you as you feel you are to that parent right now. Write "Mom" or "Dad" on it.

3. Continue this for every person who lives with you in this home.

4. With a ruler connect the helmets, thus diagraming your relationship with your family.

Next, let's make a diagram of the home (spaceship) that you visit.

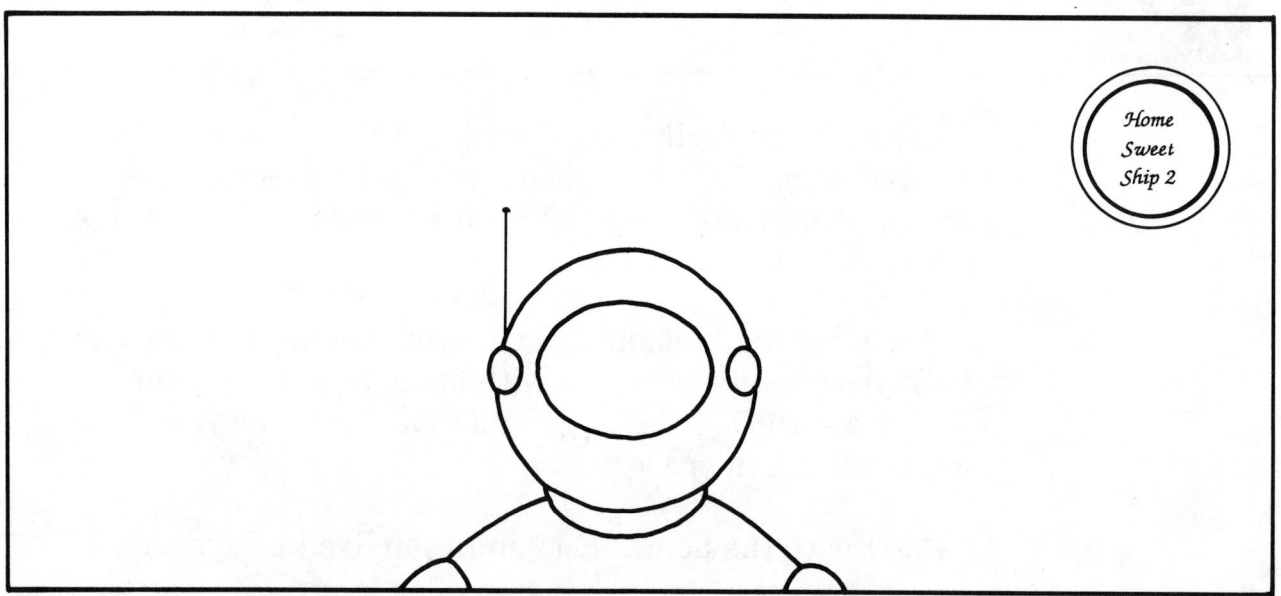

1. Write your name on the helmet provided.

2. Draw a helmet representing your non-custodial parent as close to you as you feel to that parent right now. Write "Mom" or "Dad" on it.

3. Draw helmets standing for all other people in your non-custodial home as close to you as you feel toward them. Write their names on these helmets.

4. Connect these helmets into their own diagram.

After your pictures are complete, take some time to think about them. Remember

☆ 1. These pictures are a good way to come in touch with how you feel about your family right now.

☆ 2. No feelings are bad.

☆ 3. It is better to know how you feel so that you can deal with your feelings. Keeping them all locked up inside does more harm than good.

☆ 4. Feelings change so your pictures might look different at another time.

Chapter 4
My Feelings about Myself

How You Feel about Yourself

So far in your journey through divorce you have learned a little about what divorce is,

the hills you must climb to get through your loss journey,

and the many feelings you have and will have along the way.

But the most important feeling that you have is **how you feel about yourself!!!**

This kind of feeling is known as "self-esteem." Self-esteem means how you feel about yourself as you go from person to person and day to day in your own little world. The following will help you to understand this a little better.

High self-esteem often results from nice things that others say about you or from nice things that you say and feel about yourself. Look at the examples below.

Nice things that others may have said about you	Nice things that you may have said and felt about yourself
"You are a great little artist."	"Isn't the picture that I drew neat?"
"You're a hard worker at home."	"Look how nice my room looks!"
"You are improving in math."	"I can do this math all by myself!"
"You're terrific at baseball."	"I can help you learn to catch a ball."

Write a few things that make you feel good about yourself right now.

_____

_____

# Low Self-Esteem

Besides having days when you feel *great* about yourself, you also have days when you feel not-so-good about yourself. Those are the days when things seem to go wrong for you. Pretend this was a day in your life.

You had to walk to school in the rain only to find out that somewhere between home and school you lost your lunch money. That afternoon the teacher saw that you had forgotten to do your spelling homework. When you got home, your best friend came over, but before you knew it you had a fight.

Color the picture that tells how you might feel when this kind of day happens to you.

There Is No One Else Like Me

Often little boys and girls think too much about all of the things that they do not like about themselves. This is hard on their *high self-esteem*. Let's have some fun and see just how special you really are! This page, not written on, is the same in every book. But, as soon as you start filling in the answers *you will see how special you really are!* Then, no two pages will look the same.

My name is _____ Age _____

I am a student of _____ School and am in grade _____

People I like in school are _____

At home I play with _____

I like to do the following things: (underline)

Collect things	Act in plays	Play basketball
Play baseball	Sing	Belong to a Scout troop
Dance	Perform gymnastics	Belong to the YWCA/YMCA
Write stories or poems	Belong to the 4H	Read
Ride a bicycle	Play a musical instrument	Swim
Play soccer	Draw or paint	Other _____

My biggest wish is _____

My favorite thing to do is to _____

When you are finished take some time to share a few of your answers: who you like, what you like to do, what your favorite things are. All of these are things that make you **"You."**

 # Let's Take a Closer Look at Your Ups and Downs

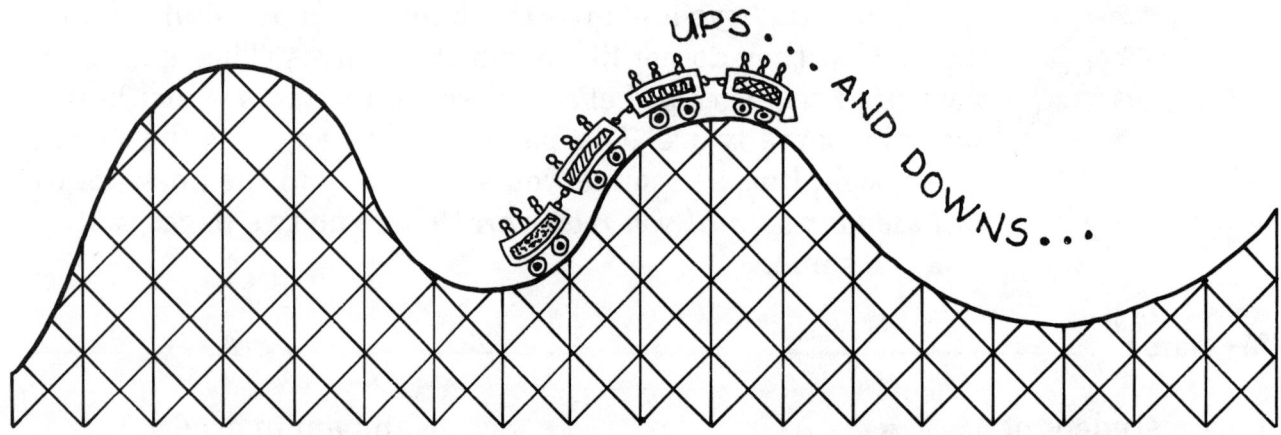

It is very important for you to learn that everyone, from little boys and girls to older grandmas and grandpas, have their up and down times in life. This is just the way life is. This has nothing to do with you being a good or bad boy or girl. You can be a good person when you feel **"up"** and a good person when you feel **"down."**

But, some children begin to feel bad about themselves when they feel "down." **This is not good**. You must always remember that even when things are hard for you,

You are still a good person,

Other people love you,

People want to help you feel better,

You must keep trying,

You can be *happy* again,

You are a very special child!!!

Your Self-esteem in Action

There is a very important lesson to learn about all of this. Whether you feel happy or sad, up or down, you have chosen to feel that way. Other people cannot force you to feel happy or sad. You decide how you are going to feel.

You will see how this is true by answering the following questions. By sharing your answers you will see that what one child might see as an **"up"** about divorce, another child might see as a **"down."**

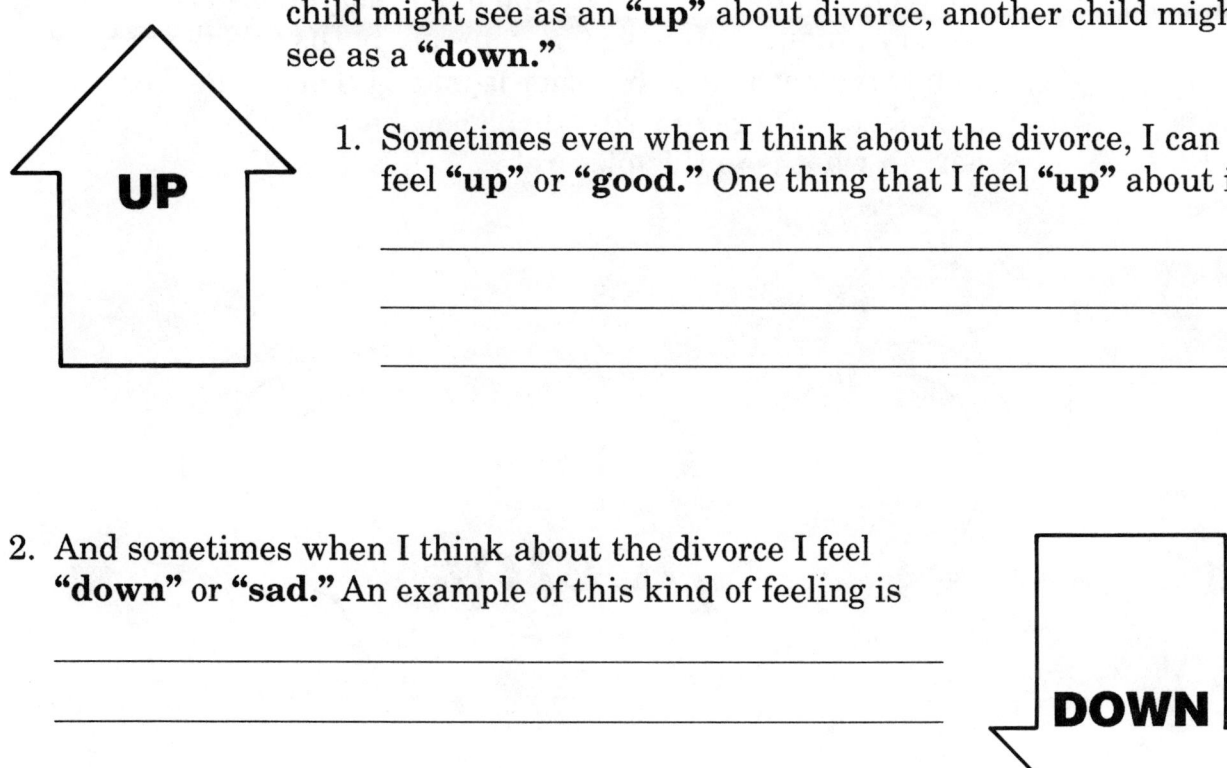

1. Sometimes even when I think about the divorce, I can feel **"up"** or **"good."** One thing that I feel **"up"** about is

   _____
   _____
   _____

2. And sometimes when I think about the divorce I feel **"down"** or **"sad."** An example of this kind of feeling is

   _____
   _____
   _____

My Special Page

As you continue on your "Loss Journey" and do page after page in your book, you will see more and more how special you are. It is time to have some fun and create a special page for yourself. Follow the dots to find out what you deserve for being so very unique. You have two separate paths to follow. One is a numbered path, and the other is made up of letters from the alphabet. Be sure to write at the bottom just why you have earned what is in this picture!

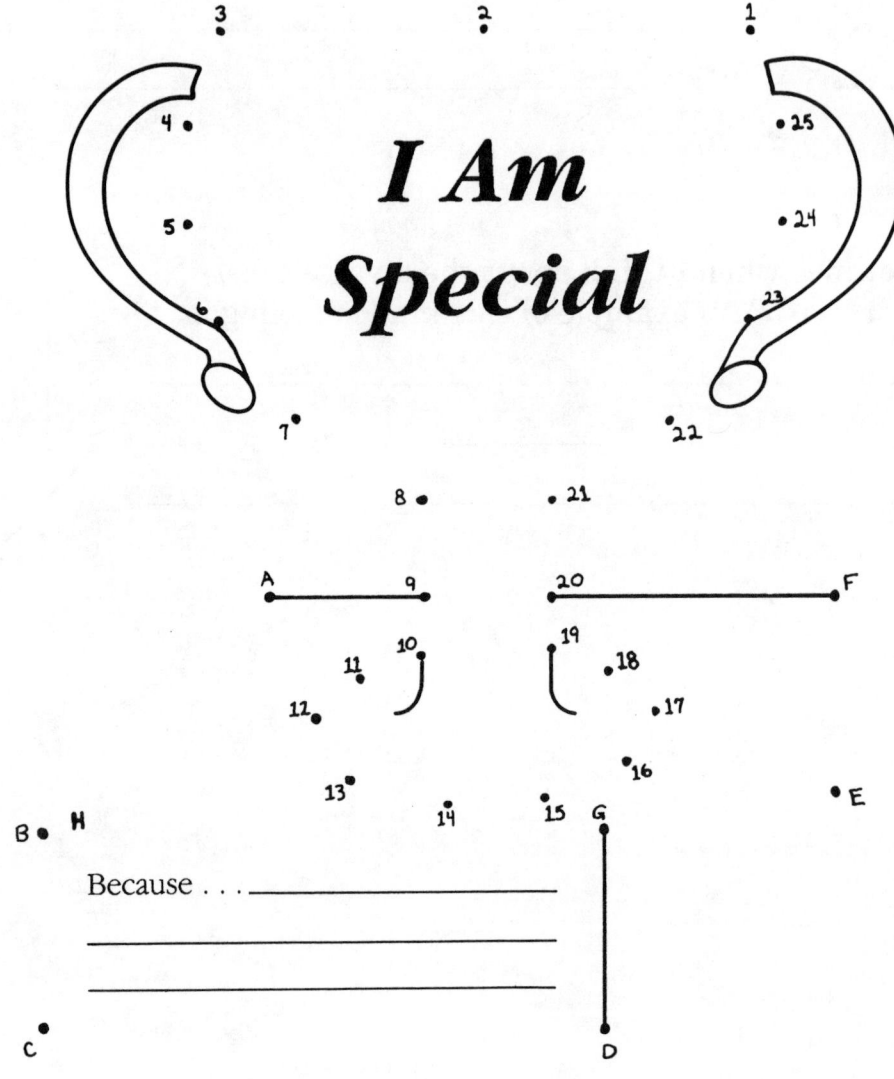

Because . . . _____

_____

_____

My Hall of Fame

Today, there are many different Halls of Fame in our country. Great football and baseball players, great inventors, and lots of other great people are recognized for their achievements in a Hall of Fame.

Well, you deserve a pat on the back, too. You have been through a crisis. You are climbing the steep hills on your Loss Journey, and you are working hard to keep up with all of your work at home and school.

Put on your thinking cap and decide what it is that you are doing very well right now. Draw a picture of it.

Chapter 5
Words I Need to Know

# Words

When divorce happens in a family, lots of other things seem to start happening, too. These things may seem scary to you because you do not understand everything going on around you—especially all the new words that you hear.

You might hear Mom and Dad talking quietly or yelling loudly about things that you do not understand. You might overhear Mom talking on the phone or Dad talking to your uncle. Almost always, there is a lot of talking about some pretty important things once Mom and Dad separate or divorce.

It is important for you to understand some of these new words so that you do not worry too much about them.

Read each definition below and find the word, in the flower, that fits the definition. Copy the word onto the line next to the definition.

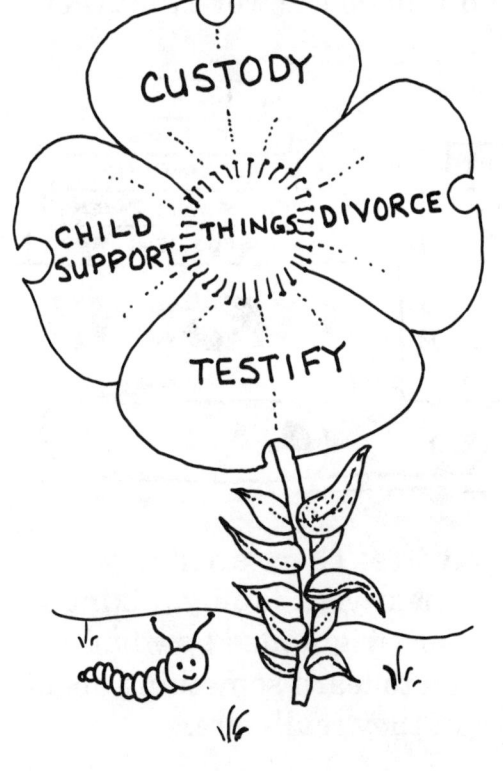

1. The lawyer tells one parent that he or she will care for and raise the child. The child will live with that parent.

   __ __ __ __ __ __ __

2. The ending of a marriage between a mom and a dad.

   __ __ __ __ __ __ __

3. When a person is called to court to tell the truth about the family getting divorced.

   __ __ __ __ __ __ __

4. The money that is needed to help raise a child.

   __ __ __ __ __

   __ __ __ __ __ __ __

49

...And More Words

Match the definitions below with the words that the train is pulling. Copy the numbers that are in front of the words being pulled onto the lines next to the corresponding definitions. Talk about them with your teacher as you do the exercise. This is a wonderful time to ask any questions that you might have about all of the new words which you are hearing.

_____ The parent with whom the child lives most of the time.

_____ The person in the courtroom who decides how and when two people will divorce.

_____ A place where a judge settles the divorce case.

_____ A child who is under the age of 18

_____ The home of the parent whom the child visits on days appointed by the judge.

_____ The parent with whom the child does *not* live most of the time.

_____ The people trained in law who help Mom and Dad do the work that they need to do in order to get a divorce.

VOCABULARY TRAIN

PLACES:
1. THE HOME OF VISITATION
2. THE COURTROOM

PERSONS:
3. THE NON-CUSTODIAL PARENT
4. THE CUSTODIAL PARENT
5. THE LAWYER
6. THE JUDGE
7. THE MINOR

These are just a few of the words that tell about divorce. There are many more. The important thing to remember is that if you hear your family talking about the divorce and you do not understand them or are frightened by what they are saying, **ask for help**. It is much better for you to learn something about the topic than it is to worry or make things worse than they really are.

My Family!

Since this chapter is shorter, it is a good time to have a little fun and get ready for the next chapter which is going to be about your family.

Sometimes children whose parents are divorced think that they do not have a family. This is very wrong!!!!

Your family is the person or persons to whom you feel the closest, with whom you feel good and comfortable. Some children's families are their moms or dads. For others, grandmas, aunts, uncles, a stepparent, etc., are the family.

Kings and queens have Coats of Arms that tell others certain things about their family. But you do not have to be royalty to have a Coat of Arms. You can create your own shield by just thinking of some neat things about you and your family and putting them in picture form on the next page.

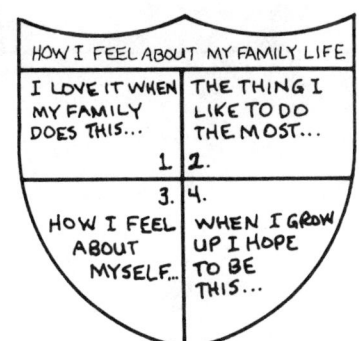

Here are some ideas to get you started on your very own shield:

1. In Box 1, draw a picture that shows you doing something with one or more members of your family that makes you very happy. This is the kind of thing that is tucked away in your memory as "one of those special times together."

2. In Box 2, draw a picture of you enjoying your favorite hobby or talent. You are an important part of your family life. If you do things that you enjoy, both you and your family will be happier.

3. In Box 3, draw a picture that shows how you feel about yourself. Maybe you see yourself as happy-go-lucky, a worry wart, moody, always giggling, etc. No matter how you act, you are an important part of your family.

4. In Box 4, put on your imagination cap and think about what you want to do when you grow up. Remember, you are special and can do just about anything you make up your mind to do.

5. In the top of the shield print a short motto that describes how you feel about your family life right now. No matter what your family is like as it goes through its ups and downs of the divorce, it is still your family and you are all very special to each other.

    Now share your shields with others who will enjoy it. You can be very proud of your family shield!

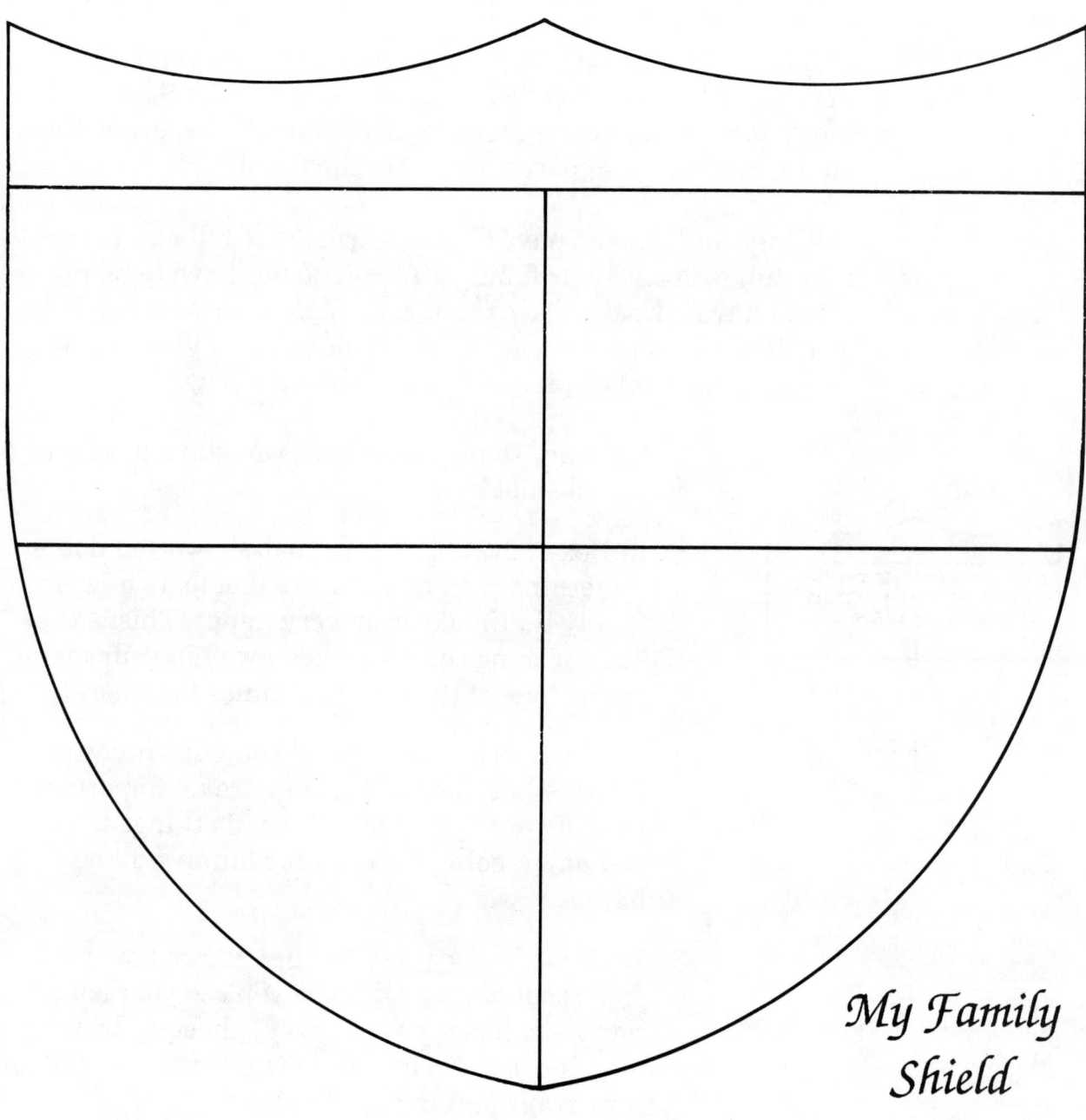

My Family Shield

Chapter 6
My Special Family

What Does Family Mean?

A long time ago when your grandma and grandpa were your age, if someone asked them what a family was, they might have said, "A family is a mom, a dad, a brother, a sister, and maybe even a little dog named Spot." That was the way most families were in those days. Of course, sometimes there were more kids in the family, and sometimes there were fewer.

There is a name for this kind of family. It is called the **traditional family**. What does such a big word mean? A tradition is something that you do again and again year after year. For example, traditions that are often done are to have turkey on Thanksgiving at Grandma and Grandpa's, and to hunt for candy on Easter.

For years and years in books, magazines, movies, and TV, the traditional family was seen in this way . . .

Mom home baking yummy treats for the kids

Dad spending his free time playing sports with the kids

Mom always being home after school

Dad having to work until suppertime

But, you know that a lot has happened to this type of family over the years:

Many moms now have jobs, so they are gone for most of the day.

Some dads even work two jobs so that their weekends are not spent fishing or playing games with their kids.

And, some moms and dads do not even live together.

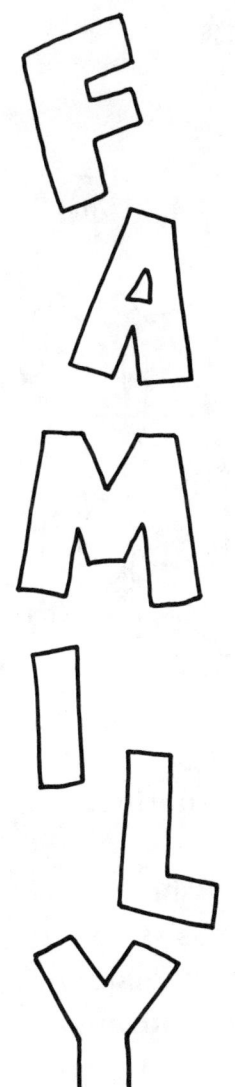

This leads us to some other kinds of family life. The first is the **extended family**. Sometimes families get bigger when a grandma or a grandpa, an Uncle Harry or an Aunt Suzie, comes to live with Mom, Dad, and the kids. This bigger family is called the extended family. If you have relatives living with you, write their names on the line.

_____

When a mom and/or a dad has separated, divorced, or died, the new kind of family created is called a **single-parent family**. In this kind of family

    All of the children might live with one parent and visit the other parent.

    Some children in the family might live with Mom while other children might live with Dad.

    All of the children might spend an equal amount of time with both parents.

Put a star ☆ next to the phrase that best describes your family situation.

The parent with whom the children live most of the time is called the **custodial parent**. This term comes from the word *custody* which means being in charge of, or caring for someone else. The parent whom the children visit on weekends or other days appointed by the judge is called the **non-custodial parent**. This parent is in charge of and takes care of the children while the children are with him or her.

After divorce or the death of a spouse, some moms and dads decide to marry again. The new form of family created is called a **stepfamily**. The new spouse who marries your mom or dad is called your stepmother or stepfather. Any children your stepmother or stepfather have are called your stepbrothers or your stepsisters. If you have a stepparent, here is a place to write that parent's name in your book.

_____

There are other kinds of family life that you will learn more about as you get older. Some children live with a **guardian**, some live in a **foster home**, while other children are **adopted**.

So you see, there are many ways to live a family life. The important thing is for you to know that you do *belong* to a family whether you live with 1, 2, 5, or 10 people. Put a star ☆ next to the paragraph(s) that best describe(s) your family. You might have more than one star.

Write *Mom* or *Dad* on the post in front of the house that best describes your family.

Change and More Change

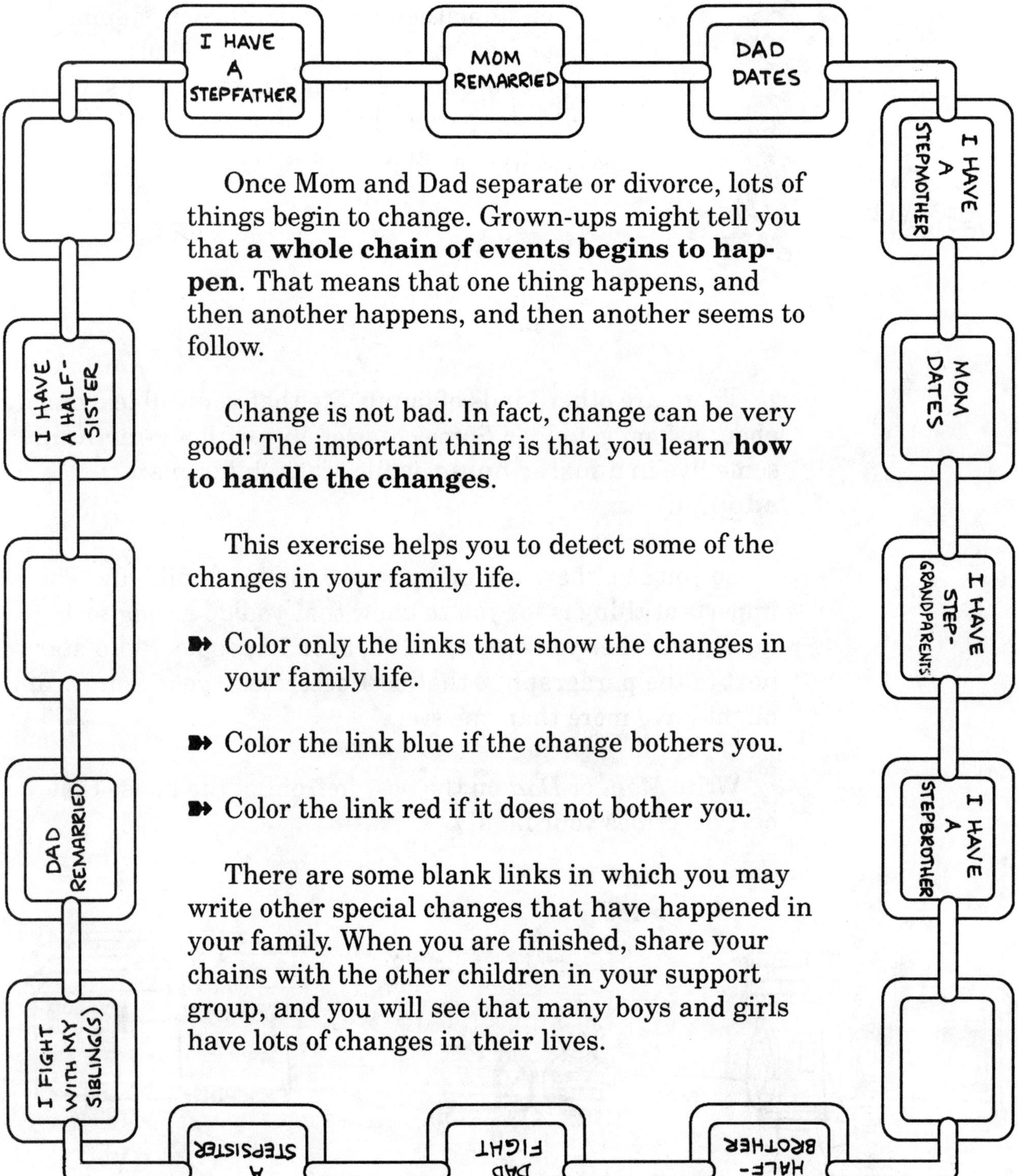

Once Mom and Dad separate or divorce, lots of things begin to change. Grown-ups might tell you that **a whole chain of events begins to happen**. That means that one thing happens, and then another happens, and then another seems to follow.

Change is not bad. In fact, change can be very good! The important thing is that you learn **how to handle the changes**.

This exercise helps you to detect some of the changes in your family life.

➡ Color only the links that show the changes in your family life.

➡ Color the link blue if the change bothers you.

➡ Color the link red if it does not bother you.

There are some blank links in which you may write other special changes that have happened in your family. When you are finished, share your chains with the other children in your support group, and you will see that many boys and girls have lots of changes in their lives.

58

A New Kind of Game that People Play

After a separation or divorce, children and parents can be so upset that they start to play games with each other. These are not fun games like Checkers or Monopoly. These games are ways a parent or child might act in order to get his or her own way or to find out some information.

Games that Some Kids Play in a Separated or Divorced Family

The **"Love Me More If I Side With You"** Game:
Some children think that one parent will love them a lot more if they take sides. So, when they are with Mom they tell stories about Dad. They think Mom will like them a lot more because they are on her side. Then, they do the same thing with Dad. This is not a good way to get close to Mom and Dad.

The **"Get This Or Do That For Me So I Will Love You"** Game:
Sometimes in a divorce children feel they do not get enough attention. So, they try to bribe Mom or Dad to buy them something or to do something special for them. Most moms and dads do not feel really loved when they are bribed, and lots of times the children begin to feel guilty over bribing them.

The **"But Mommy, Daddy Said I Could"** Game:
Sometimes when a child is mad at one parent, the child will try to trick that parent by making him or her feel mean. If Mom says it is time to go to bed and the child does not want to go, the child might say, "Daddy said I could go to bed anytime I want to." Playing such tricks does not make most children feel very good, and Mom and Dad have a hard time believing what is really true.

Games Parents Play in a Separated or Divorced Family

The **"You Spy"** or **"Tattle-tale"** Game:

Some divorced parents get very upset with their ex-wife or ex-husband. While they were married they knew a lot about each other, but now they do not. So, sometimes a parent will use the children to find out what is going on with the other parent. Spying or having to tattle is very hard on children for they do not feel loyal to the parent they must tell on. You must tell your parents that you love them both but cannot be their spy.

The **"Tug-of-War"** Game:

This is another game that some children are forced to play. Both parents want the child on their side. The children only feel caught in the middle. You must tell your parents that you love them both and that you do not want to be a part of their fights.

How to Stop Playing These Games

One way to stop playing these games is to understand why you played them in the first place. If you broke your leg you would use crutches until your leg healed and became stronger.

Well, these games are sometimes played when you and your parents are hurting a lot after the separation or divorce. The games are like crutches to help you get through your rough time. But, as you get stronger, you should throw them away. Remember

☆   1. Such games can hurt people you love.

☆   2. It is better to talk over your feelings with Mom and Dad than to play games.

☆   3. Let Mom and Dad know that you do not want to be in the middle of their fights.

☆   4. If you all stop playing these hurtful games, you will come to love each other in a better way.

The Challenge of Living in Two Families

On this page is a house that is divided down the middle. This is one way of showing how you go back and forth living between two places.

You will see words written on the houses. Take turns reading the different phrases aloud, and discuss them with your teacher. Then outline in color the words that fit your family. Put a star ☆ next to the ones that bother you right now.

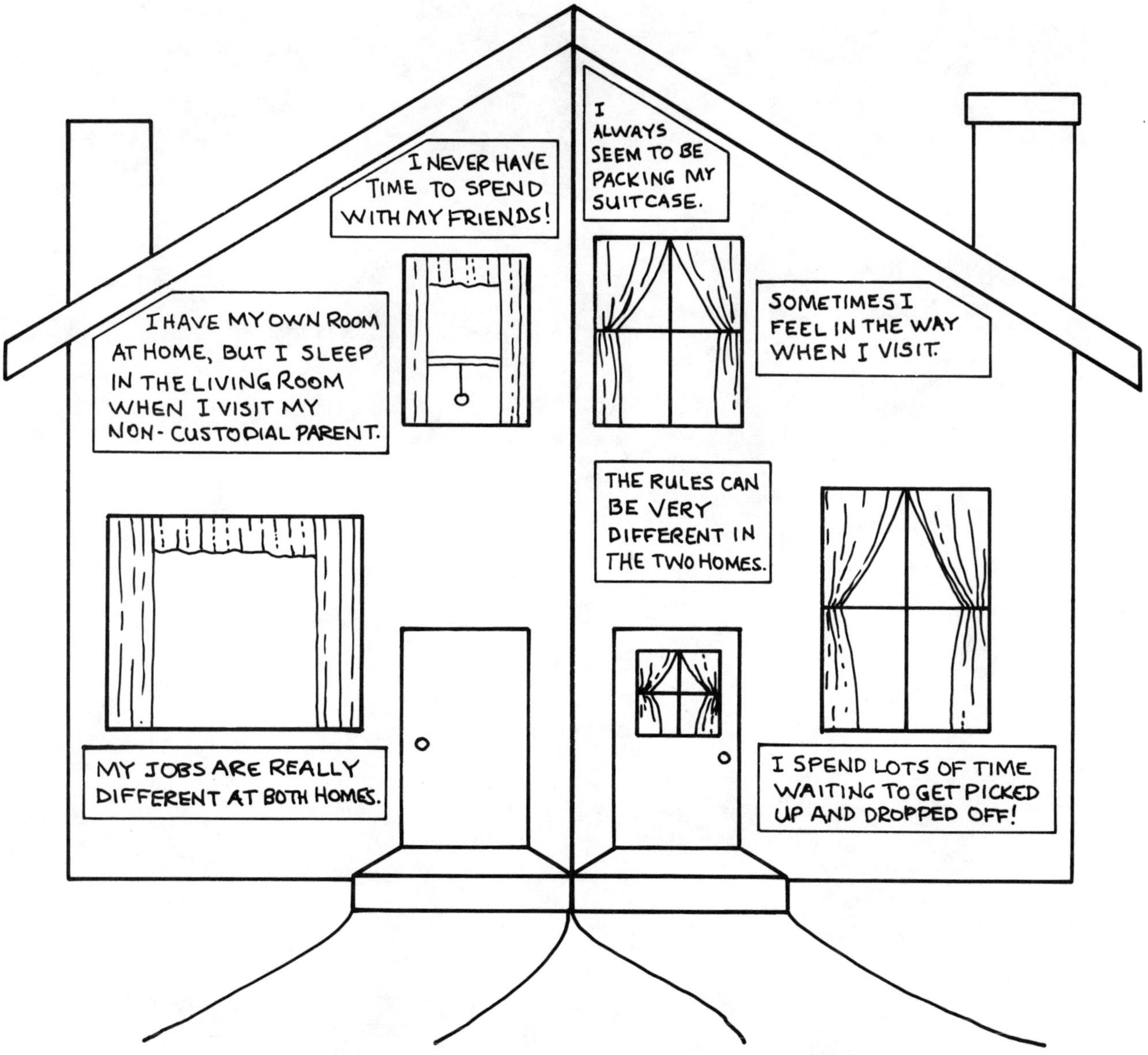

- I NEVER HAVE TIME TO SPEND WITH MY FRIENDS!
- I ALWAYS SEEM TO BE PACKING MY SUITCASE.
- I HAVE MY OWN ROOM AT HOME, BUT I SLEEP IN THE LIVING ROOM WHEN I VISIT MY NON-CUSTODIAL PARENT.
- SOMETIMES I FEEL IN THE WAY WHEN I VISIT.
- THE RULES CAN BE VERY DIFFERENT IN THE TWO HOMES.
- MY JOBS ARE REALLY DIFFERENT AT BOTH HOMES.
- I SPEND LOTS OF TIME WAITING TO GET PICKED UP AND DROPPED OFF!

61

Chapter 7
Divorce and the School

Divorce and School?

You might be asking yourself "What does divorce have to do with school? Mom and Dad are the ones who are getting divorced, not Mom and the school or Dad and the school."

You are right in one way; the divorce is between Mom and Dad. But, you have also learned that divorce can create lots of feelings in you. When you come to school with all of those feelings running around in your mind and heart, it can be very hard to keep up with your schoolwork.

Let's take a look at what happens. Remember, divorce is a crisis, and during a crisis many things feel out-of-control. Lots of things can happen that change the way children act when they come to school, especially if they are upset.

<u>Underline</u>, in color, the parts of the following lists that describe where you are in school right now. Also, <u>underline</u> how you have been feeling and behaving.

Grades:
Sometimes grades go way down because the child feels bad and gives up.

Homework is often not done well since so many other things happen at night.

Some kids are mad, so they get bad grades to make Mom or Dad mad.

Children often decide to make school their "happy" place, so they work hard and raise their grades.

Feelings and Behavior:

Angry children may act mean toward, or pick on, other children and teachers.

Sad children often can hardly work or play.

Frightened children may "hang" onto the teacher all day, following the teacher around and tattling on other children.

Lonely kids sometimes stay away from everyone in order to avoid ever talking about the divorce.

Nervous children may worry so much about money and their families that they do not think about their schoolwork enough.

Tired children lose interest in school.

Maybe they have lost sleep:

> eavesdropping at night
>
> > worrying
> >
> > > being afraid that something will happen to their other parent.

Feeling sick a lot can keep children from working in school. When some children are very sad, they feel "real" or "imagined" headaches, stomach aches, etc.

Dreamland:

Some kids use school as an escape from their upsets. They go to their desks and

stare into space,

> hold their heads all day,
>
> > ignore their teachers,
> >
> > > skip their work.

This is not a good kind of daydreaming. It can become a nightmare when little or none of the schoolwork is done.

By looking over the lines that you have colored, you will be able to learn more about yourself and how you perform in school. This will help your teachers and parents know more about how you are feeling. They will be able to help you get through the rough times a little more easily.

How Can School Help You through a Divorce?

Look at the ways school can help you through the ups and downs of divorce.

Star ☆ in color the phrases that show how you feel in school right now.

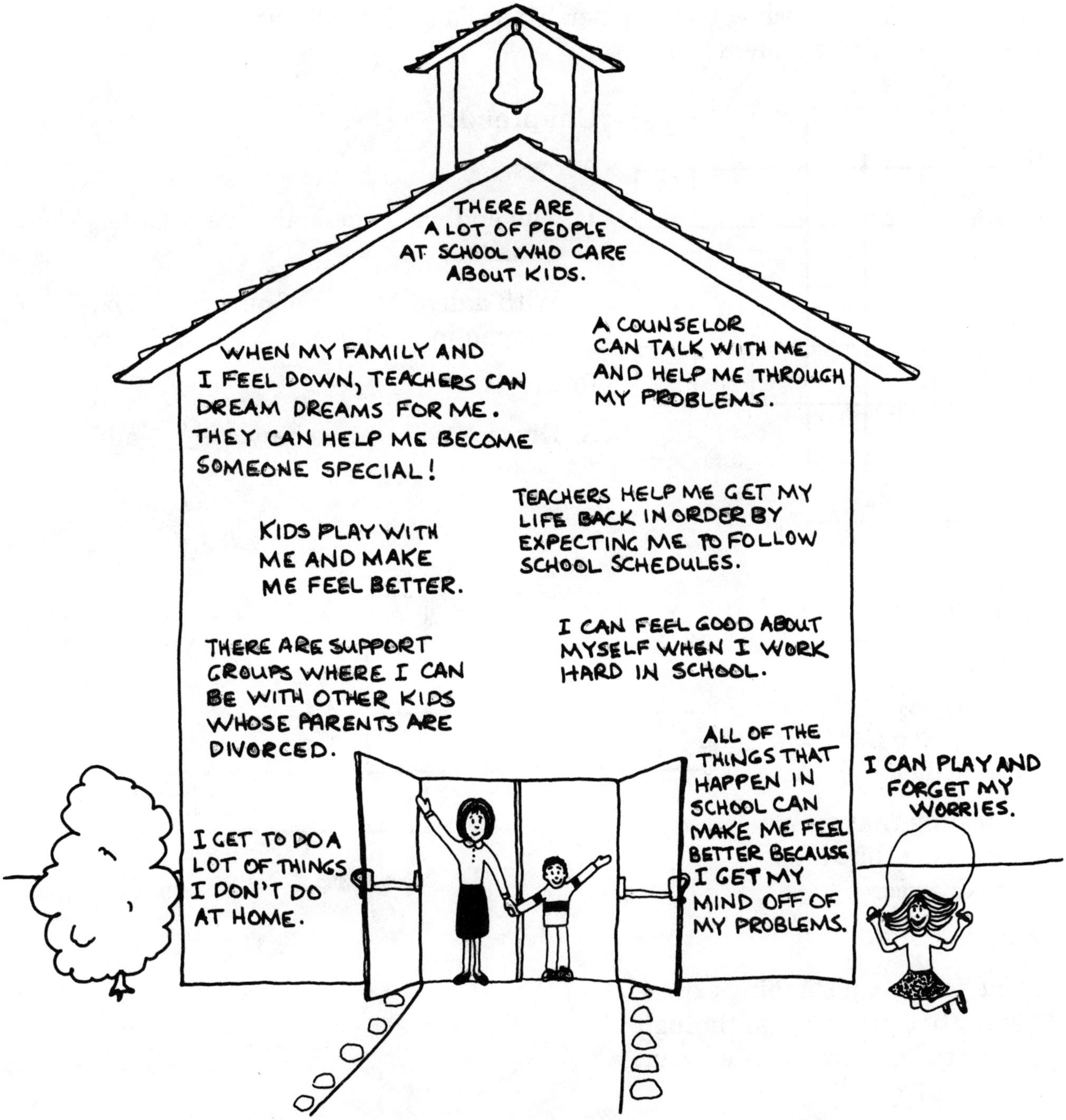

- THERE ARE A LOT OF PEOPLE AT SCHOOL WHO CARE ABOUT KIDS.
- WHEN MY FAMILY AND I FEEL DOWN, TEACHERS CAN DREAM DREAMS FOR ME. THEY CAN HELP ME BECOME SOMEONE SPECIAL!
- A COUNSELOR CAN TALK WITH ME AND HELP ME THROUGH MY PROBLEMS.
- KIDS PLAY WITH ME AND MAKE ME FEEL BETTER.
- TEACHERS HELP ME GET MY LIFE BACK IN ORDER BY EXPECTING ME TO FOLLOW SCHOOL SCHEDULES.
- I CAN FEEL GOOD ABOUT MYSELF WHEN I WORK HARD IN SCHOOL.
- THERE ARE SUPPORT GROUPS WHERE I CAN BE WITH OTHER KIDS WHOSE PARENTS ARE DIVORCED.
- ALL OF THE THINGS THAT HAPPEN IN SCHOOL CAN MAKE ME FEEL BETTER BECAUSE I GET MY MIND OFF OF MY PROBLEMS.
- I CAN PLAY AND FORGET MY WORRIES.
- I GET TO DO A LOT OF THINGS I DON'T DO AT HOME.

Review

Every day you learn new things in school. There are books, lessons, tests, computers, etc. But, every so often you must stop and review the things that you have learned just to see how much you remember. This chapter is a good place to do just that. Here are some mini-crossword puzzles. See how much you remember. There is a puzzle for each of the first six chapters.

Chapter 1:

Across:

1. The ending of the marriage between Mom and Dad.

2. With a divorce, lots of new things begin to happen in our lives.

Down:

A. Divorce takes place between ____ and ____.

Chapter 2:

Across:

1. A very big problem that is too hard to solve alone.

2. A feeling that we have for a long time after the divorce.

Down:

A. The mountain climbing experience that you must go through after the divorce is called your "___ Journey."

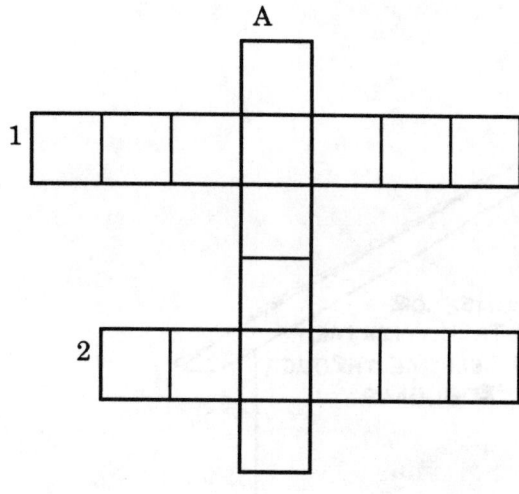

68

Chapter 3:

Across:

1. A feeling that means the same as "bubbly" or "excited."

2. The feeling that shows you care and feel close to another person.

Down:

A. To feel weak and not able to do something.

B. To feel sad or down-in-the dumps.

Chapter 4:

Across:

1. The way that you feel about yourself is called your_____-esteem.

2. A day when you feel "high" and things are going your way can be called an_____day.

3. A "down" day when lots of things seem to go wrong can be called one of your_____days.

Down:

A. There is no one else on earth just like you. That makes you a very_____child.

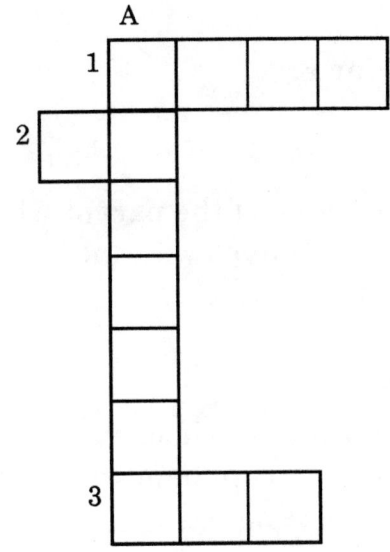

Chapter 5:

Across:

1. The place where your Mom, Dad, and their lawyers meet the judge about the divorce.

2. The person trained in law to help your Mom and Dad with their divorce.

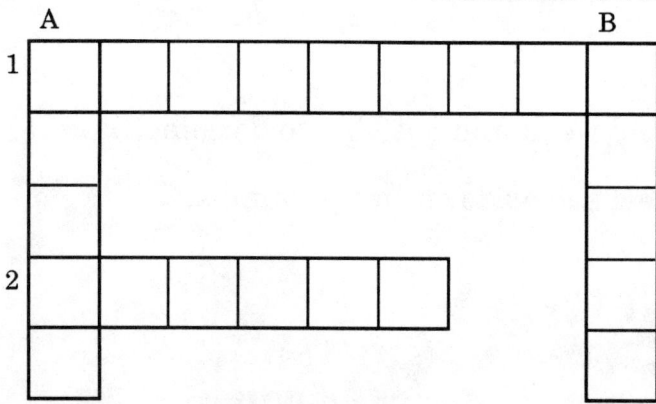

Down:

A. The money given to the custodial parent to help pay for the needs of the children is called _____ support.

B. Any child under the age of 18 is called a _____.

Chapter 6:

Across:

1. The name of the parent who the child lives with most of the time.

Down:

A. The whole chain of events that begins to happen after a divorce is called _____.

B. A game played by Mom and Dad where both try to pull the child to their side.

C. Lots of games are played by children in order to try to get their mom or dad to _____ them better.

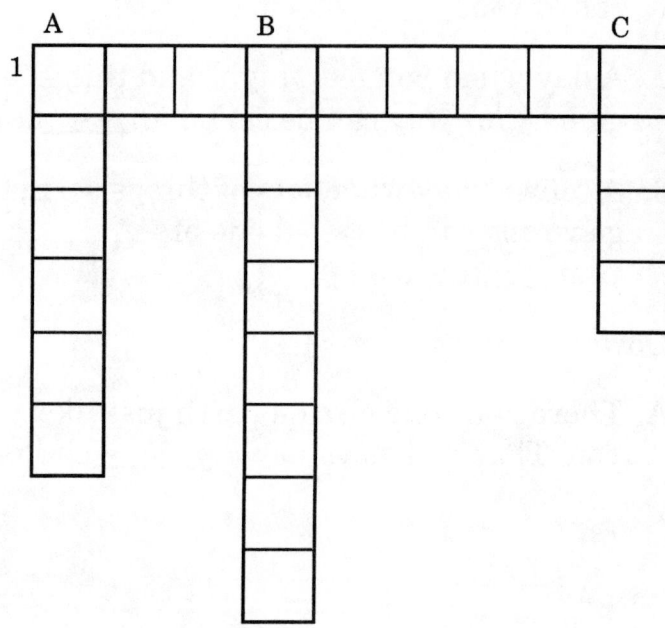

It's Time to Enter the Wonderful . . .

School and books go together but there are many other kinds of books besides reading, math, and science books, and other textbooks.

Story books are filled with lots and lots of information about life. Here are some reasons why books are helpful when you are going through a hard time.

They can . . .

- Teach you lots of things about divorce
- Help you meet other boys and girls whose parents are divorced
- Show you how other children handle their problems
- Be great friends
- Always be there for you
- Never get mad or leave you
- Make you laugh and cry and feel lots of different ways
- Give you fun things to talk about with your friends

As you read a book you should try to do *three things*. This helps to make the book even more fun for you.

☆ Pretend you are one of the people in the book!

☆ Let yourself feel the way that person is feeling!

☆ Try to learn a good lesson from the book!

Hop on the book worm and travel through the next few pages where you can learn about some wonderful books for children about divorce. These pages are mostly for your parent(s) so that they can take you to the library. Make sure that you show these pages to them.

Fun with Books
An Annotated Bibliography for Preschool through Grade Three

Ages:

4-8   Baum. *One More Time.* New York: Morrow, 1986.

This little story tells about the joys and fears of Simon's visiting days with his dad. After spending a wonderful Sunday together, Simon gets anxious when it is time to say goodbye. This story is an excellent way to help parents and children open up this stressful topic for discussion.

7-10   Berger. *A Friend Can Help.* Chicago: Childrens' Press, 1974.

In this book a child psychologist helps an eight-year-old girl whose parents are divorced to open up and talk things out with a friend. Full page photos show the many emotions and moods which can be felt during such a crisis.

8-12   Berger. *How Does It Feel When Your Parents Get Divorced?* New York: J. Messner, 1977.

This story with photos grasps the dynamics of the emotions of an eight-year-old child who is experiencing divorce in her family. This very touching book discusses these problems and emotions through the eyes and heart of a young child whose life story has changed significantly because of her parents' divorce.

4-8   Boegehold. *Daddy Doesn't Live Here Anymore: A Book about Divorce.* New York: Golden Press, 1985.

Darling little Casey finds herself so sad over all of the fighting going on between her mommy and daddy. She sees that Dad is gone more and more, and Mom is crying more and more. Finally, one day, she is told that although both Mom and Dad love Casey very much, they do not love each other and will be getting a divorce. The story unfolds showing Casey's reactions which range from crying to trying to bring them together again, to taking the blame on herself, to even trying to run away. With the love and support of her parents, Casey learns how to live her new family life.

1-3   Brown, M. *The Dead Bird.* Reading, Mass.: Addison-Wesley, 1965.

This is a touching story of several children who come upon a little bird that had recently died. Facts about death are interwoven within the plot. The children learn certain physical characteristics of death such as—the body stiffens, gets cold, there is not a heartbeat. The children decide to care for the dead bird just like adults do when someone dies. They decide on a nice funeral, dig a grave, collect plants and flowers, and show their feelings by singing a song and crying. The various stages of grief are simplistically incorporated and treated well. They experience sorrow, share grief, and look for support until finally time gradually heals their pain.

5-10   Brown. *Dinosaurs Divorce: A Guide for Changing Families.* Boston: Little, Brown & Co., 1986.

This delightful book is composed of marvelous illustrations portraying many of the major areas involved in divorce and family life as seen by young children. And, it is all done through clever little dinosaur characters who captivate the young readers. Profound topics such as what leads to divorce, feelings related to divorce, visitation days, celebrating holidays in two places, parents dating and remarrying, etc., are all explored. Children of all ages love this book.

3-7	Caines. *Daddy*. New York: Harper & Row, 1977.

This little story emphasizes the special relationship that exists between Windy and her dad. Even though Windy gets wrinkles in her stomach during the week when she worries about her dad, they immediately disappear when he arrives early Saturday morning for their day together. The story very beautifully shows that the noncustodial parent need not buy his or her way into the heart of the child.

6-8	Conta and Reardon. *Feelings Between Kids and Parents*. Chicago: Childrens Press, 1974.

Fourteen parent/child situations are briefly presented, each accompanied by a full-page colored photograph. Following the explanation of the "feeling situation," key questions are asked that may stimulate sharing between parent and child.

6-9	Dragonwagon. *Always, Always*. New York: MacMillan, 1984.

Beautiful full-page pictures highlight a tender story of a young girl who learns how to treasure special memories from both her home with Mom in New York and her home with Dad in Colorado. Her parents worked very hard to show her that even though they were divorced, their love for her would go on—always.

3-8	Girard. *At Daddy's on Saturdays*. Niles, Ill.: A. Whitman, 1987.

Katie's mom and dad are separated and will soon be divorced. The author clearly presents to the reader all of the worries, changes, and reactions of a young child to divorce. Any parent reading this book to a child would see the importance of divorced parents respecting each other and working together for the sake of the child.

3-6	Goff. *Where Is Daddy?: The Story of a Divorce*. Boston: Beacon, 1969.

This is a touching story which will help guide parents (who are themselves struggling with great pain and confusion) to take an overwhelmingly puzzling event and break it down to manageable size for their children. Through the character of little Janeydear, sensitive areas regarding divorce are treated. Such a tender story can serve as a mirror reflecting the problems common to many families.

4-8	Grollman. *Talking about Divorce and Separation: A Dialogue Between Parent and Child*. Boston: Beacon, 1975.

This book is a two-part guide to helping small children of divorcing parents face the reality and consequences of family break-up. It contains an illustrated children's "read along" section that can help open the door to dealing with the difficult subject of divorce for a child. It also includes sources for further help and a bibliography of fiction and nonfiction about divorce.

3-7	Hazen. *Two Homes to Live In: A Child's-Eye View of Divorce*. New York: Human Sciences Press, 1978.

Niki, a young girl, explains how she comes to terms with her parents' divorce. She learns that parents, not children, divorce. She also realizes that the children are not to blame and that it is normal to have the fears and dreams which she experiences. This book deals with the idea that there are big adjustments to be made as parents separate and divorce, but slowly these adjustments can be made as others offer their love and support.

8-10	Hurwitz. *DeDe Takes Charge!* New York: Morrow, 1984.

DeDe is a delightful young girl who the reader easily comes to love. She is in the middle of her divorced parents, trying to do what many children do—please both Mom and Dad. This is a challenge since Dad demands perfection while Mom is anything but perfect. Even with such different parents, DeDe knows that they both love her and want to take care of her, each in his/her own way.

5-8   Lisker. *Two Special Cards*. New York: Harcourt Brace Jovanovich, 1976.

Both the story and the large descriptive pictures do an excellent job of conveying key issues in the life of an eight-year-old child whose parents are divorcing. The greatest emphasis in the book lies in the gradual transition of living in two different places, showing that it is possible to love each parent very specially, and, in turn, to be loved deeply by separated or divorced parents.

2-4   Mann, P. *My Dad Lives in a Downtown Hotel*. Garden City, N.Y.: Doubleday, 1973.

The author beautifully presents the feelings of a young boy after his parents' divorce. For Joey, divorce means guilt, hopes for reunion, shame over not having a dad in his home, anger at his dad, and sadness for his mom. The author takes this painful situation and shows that it does not have to be the end of the world, for Joey is able to use his creativity to help find answers to his problems. Although there is some fantasy in his solutions, the book is filled with great insight into childrens' feelings.

7-9   Newfield. *A Book for Jodan*. New York: Atheneum, 1975.

Jodan lived her nine young years in an almost too-good-to-be-true way, sharing in so many fun activities that she and her parents did together. It was such a shock to her when these events were replaced with tension, quarrels, loud arguments, and finally separation. Jodan did not even get to see her dad since she lived in California and he lived in Massachusetts. The author sensitively and creatively presents an idea whereby a parent and child can capture precious moments to treasure during times when they are apart and lonely. A scrapbook made by both Dad and Jodan encompasses every level of human development. Indeed, just reading this book can serve as a source of many helpful ideas to parents and children alike.

6-9   Paris. *Mom Is Single*. Chicago: Childrens' Press, 1980.

This story with full-page color photos, portrays a seven-year-old boy's feelings about his parents' divorce. The story presents many of the common experiences children learn to cope with when living with single working moms. The anger and insecurity arising from questions such as "Why did things have to change?" "Could Mom leave, too?" "Is Daddy lonely?", etc., are resolved through talking things out and coming to understand that just because Mom and Dad do not live together does not mean that they do not care about their child.

3-5   Perry. *Mommy and Daddy Are Divorced*. New York: Dial, 1978.

Joey and Ned work hard at trying to understand why Daddy and Mommy divorced. They ask questions in order to try and learn about their new way of living. Although there are times when they are sad, there are also times when they share very happy moments in their new family life.

5-8   Schuchman. *Two Places to Sleep*. Minneapolis: Carolrhoda, 1979.

Seven-year-old David describes what it is like living with his dad and visiting his mom on weekends. Interwoven in the story are the adjustments needed as a result of divorce. This book also explores everyday things parents and children can do to strengthen their relationship. Divorce is seen as something you do not like but cannot change. The story clearly emphasizes that the child is not the cause of the divorce.

K-2   Stein, S. *On Divorce: An Open Family Book for Parents and Children Together*. New York: Walker, 1979.

This unique presentation of a child's book on divorce can be used in a variety of ways. The format of its forty-seven pages is generally done is this manner: one page is a black-and-white photograph of either Becky, her parents, or her two little friends. The opposite page has 1/2" print telling the storyline for the child along with small print with a great deal of information for the parent. The latter analyzes the primary story and gives practical recommendations for the adult.

3-7   Stinson. *Mom and Dad Don't Live Together Anymore*. Toronto: Annick, 1984.

The little girl in this story teaches young and old alike about the many thoughts and worries children have about divorce. By looking at the pictures and reading about the child's concerns, the reader will learn that children can come to know that Mom and Dad love them dearly although they no longer love each other.

6-8   Thomas. *Eliza's Daddy*. New York: Harcourt Brace Jovanovich, 1976.

Eliza would yearn for Saturdays when her dad would visit her. They would go wherever Eliza suggested. She was a little jealous over her daddy's new family which consisted of a new wife, a stepdaughter Eliza's age and a baby boy. After some troubled dreams, she finally got up enough nerve to ask to visit his new home. What a pleasant time that was.

5-8   Vigna. *Grandma without Me*. Niles, Ill.: A. Whitman, 1984.

This story superbly treats the topic of grandparents and grandchildren being separated due to a divorce. Colorful pictures and a touching story show how a grandma and her darling little grandson remain very close even though they cannot see each other. A scrapbook holds their special moments which they will share when they see each other again.

4-8   Vigna. *Mommy and Me By Ourselves Again*. Niles, Ill.: A. Whitman, 1987.

The author, in a few pages, treats several major areas of stress in the life of a child from a divorced family. Amy's dad never comes to visit her and this hurts her a lot. Amy's mom was dating a man who was kind to Amy, but the romance ended and Amy lost again. Soft pictures and carefully chosen words help the reader to learn that with love and support, children can heal from such situations.

1-3   Viorst, J. *The Tenth Good Thing about Barney*. New York: Atheneum, 1971.

This classic little story about a boy's pet cat that dies helps to walk a child through the stages of loss. The little boy's mom and dad support him a lot during his time of sorrow. He is so sad he can't even eat or watch TV. Together the family plans a funeral for Barney. Dad tells his son to think of ten good things about Barney which can be told at the funeral. Through this experience the little boy learns that life is not wasted by death, but death helps to contribute to new life.

K-3   Wilt, J. *Handling Your Ups and Downs*. Waco, Tex.: Educational Products Division World, 1979.

Handling Your Ups and Downs is a delightful book for young readers covering a wide range of emotions which children experience during their good and bad times. The author, through art and well-chosen words, explains to children what happens as they move from one emotion to another. Grief, loneliness, anger, guilt, security, and many more feelings are understood as the children are walked through simple exercises and clearly developed terms.

K-2   Zolotow, C. *My Grandson Lew*. New York: Harper and Row, 1974.

The depth and beauty of this little five-minute story is difficult to adequately describe. Zolotow masterfully teaches parents the importance of supporting their children through a grandparent's death rather than pretending it never happened. The reader learns, through the eyes of a little boy, just how many treasured memories children have from their early years. And when these memories are about a deceased grandparent, how much better it is to be able to share these with your parent rather than both parent and child suffering alone and silently.

K-3 Zolotow, C. *The Quarreling Book.* New York: Harper and Row, 1963.

When Mr. James started the day by forgetting to kiss his wife good-bye one morning, a bad mood started in the family that ended up spreading all the way to the children's school. This short little story lets children learn how a simple little thing can turn a big, bad mood around in a family. Since many families experiencing loss have lots of bad moods to handle, this story is excellent to use as an opener for any group session with children. It will never be outdated.

Chapter 8
Little Tugs-of-War Inside Me

 # My Mixed-up Feelings

Did you ever wish you could take all of the things in your mind and heart that seem mixed-up over the divorce and make them right again? That is a pretty normal feeling. You have already learned about the many changes that can happen after a divorce. Sometimes so many things are running around inside of your head, it can seem like you have your own little storm swirling around inside of you.

Blocks and More Blocks

There are several meanings for the word *Block*. First, remember hearing about the "blocker" in football. Well, you have something like a little "blocker" inside of your mind that wants to push away all of your heartaches. This little "blocker" does not want you to "face" your problems. It says, "If you ignore your troubles, they will go away."

NO, NO, NO! This does not work. If things keep piling up, they just get harder and harder to handle.

Second, remember the little blocks that you played with as a baby that had the alphabet on them? You stacked them up and knocked them down. In a way you can still find yourself playing with blocks when you get older. Some children build make-believe walls out of blocks that they hide behind. Each block is a different problem.

Look at the wall that these children are hiding behind. Color any block that tells what you might be doing to run away from your problems. Fill in the empty blocks with something else that you might do to run from your problems.

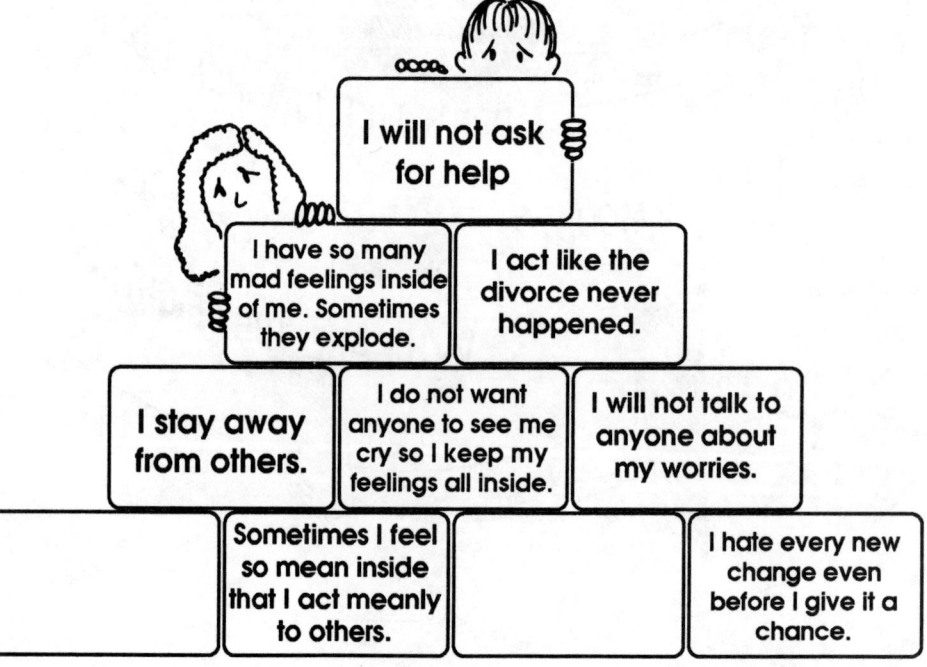

80

Remember:

☆ 1. Changes can be hard for you because you can be afraid of new things.

☆ 2. Building a wall to hide behind is natural.

☆ 3. If you stay behind the wall, you must go through your problems alone.

☆ 4. It is better to let others help you take down your wall, block by block.

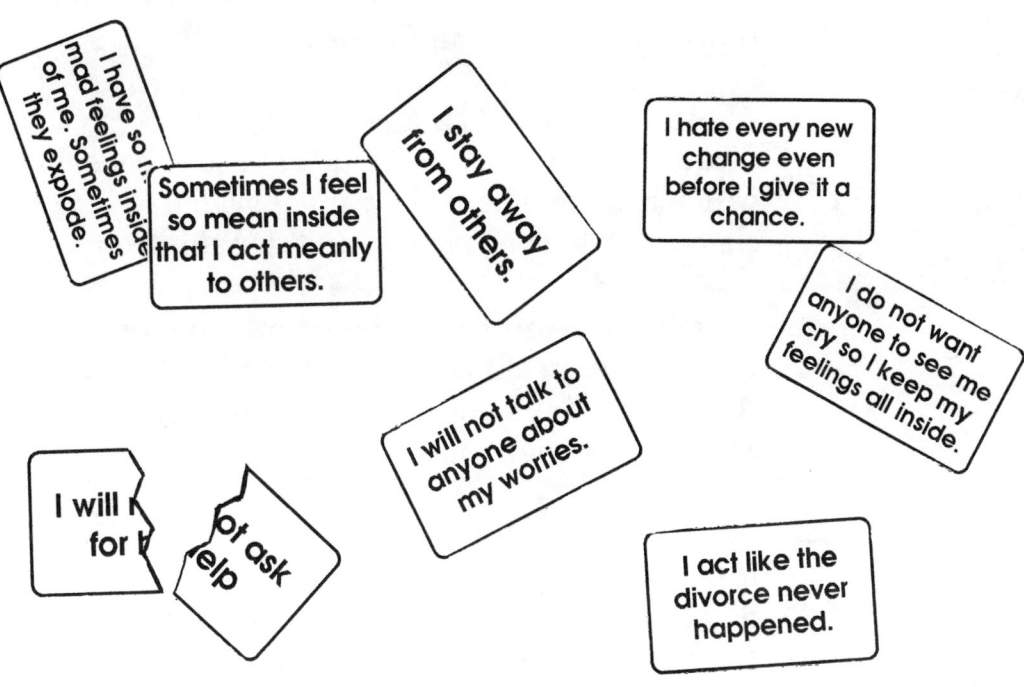

Does Anyone Know the Problems I Have?

Everyone in a family that is getting divorced has problems. Some of the problems are real and some are imagined. The first important step in helping yourself feel better is to realize what is bothering you. The second important step is to then let someone help you with your problems.

Here are a few of the things that bother kids a lot. Put a check ✓ on the line in front of your problem(s).

_____ **Being afraid that you might be left alone**
Sometimes after one parent leaves, children fear that their other parent might also leave them.

_____ **Avoid playing with the other kids**
Some children are so afraid that other boys and girls will ask them where their mom or dad is that they choose not to ever play with other children.

_____ **Letting out anger at the wrong parent**
Every so often children are so mad at one parent that they let all their angry feelings out at the other parent. This causes even more bad feelings.

_____ **Thinking you have to get Mom and Dad back together**
Some children worry and worry thinking up ways to get Mom and Dad back together. They will even make up stories to get one parent to like the other again.

_____ **Being bad to get attention**
Some moms and dads are so tired and upset during a divorce that the kids often feel that they are not loved anymore because they do not get as much attention as they used to. So, they often do bad things, like getting bad grades or breaking something in order to get attention.

These are just a few of the problems children can have. Here is space to write in one of your problems that is not already listed.

_____

_____

_____

_____

Do not forget:

☆ 1. Sometimes the problem is not as bad as you imagine it to be.

☆ 2. No problem is too big for you to get help with.

☆ 3. There is always someone near who can help you.

☆ 4. Never be afraid to ask for help.

How to Feel Closer and Happier When You Are with Mom or Dad

Building "mental blocks" and worrying about problems can really wear you down. It can almost seem that these struggles are like little wars going on inside of you. One part of you wants to be **happy-go-lucky** and another part just feels **down-in-the-dumps**. What do you do?

A good place to start is to think of some things which you can do for Mom and Dad that make them and you feel really good inside. Color the squares on the balloon that describe what you do to feel close to Mom or Dad. In some of the blank squares write your own words that tell of special things you do that Mom or Dad love.

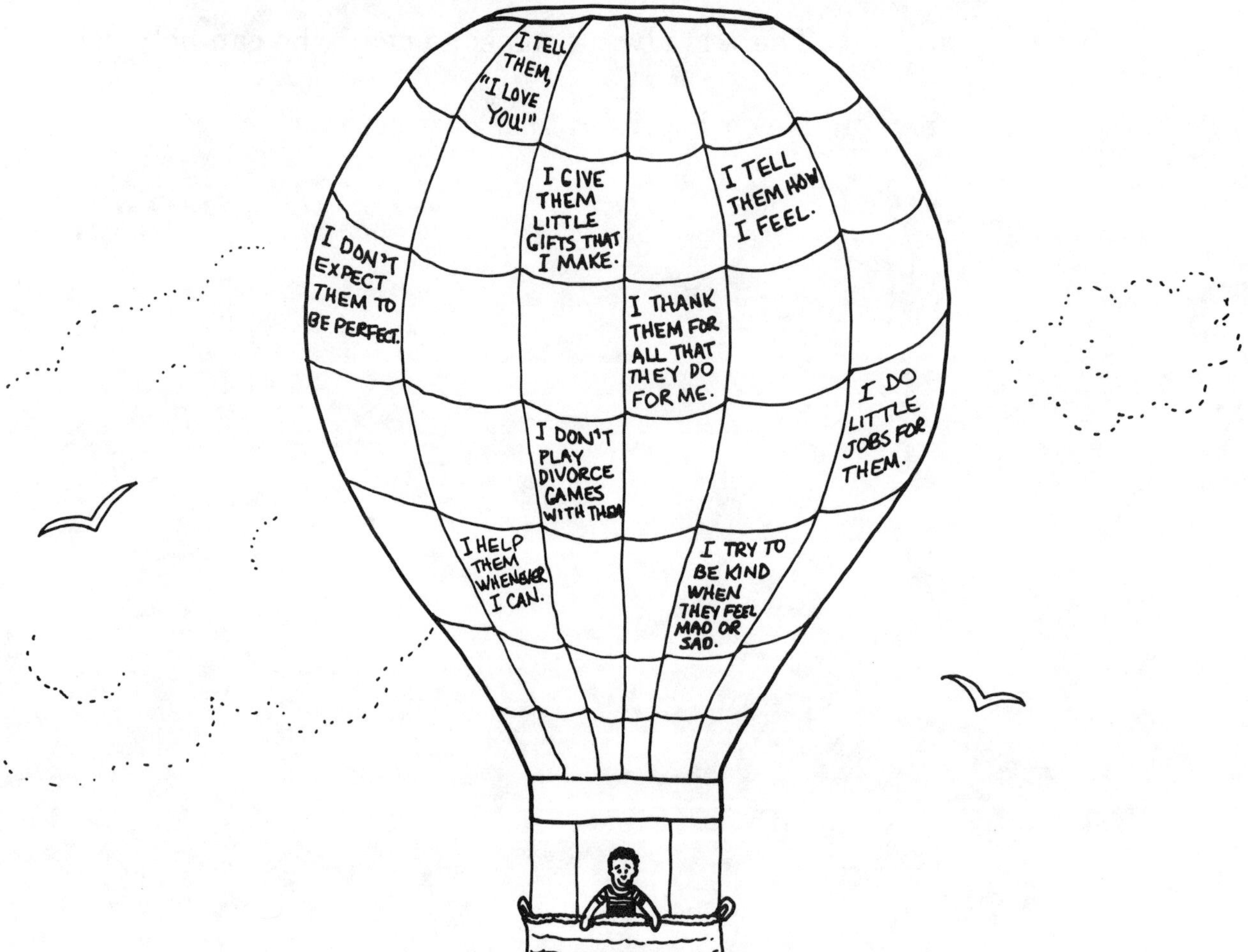

Feeling Better Again

One thing that you learned so far is that it is normal to have some ups and downs when those little wars are going on inside of you. But, there is one more very important thing for you to learn. If you decide to be down-in-the-dumps, you will stay there. Only **one person** can choose to make you feel better, and that person is **you**. How can you do that? The next exercise is a good place to begin.

1. Print your first name on the shirt in the picture below. This will remind you that you are in charge of making yourself as happy as you can!

2. Study the headings on each line. Choose the ones that would make you feel better if you did them on a "down day."

3. Write examples of those headings on the lines. (Reading: sports stories, comic books, etc. Outdoors: biking, hiking, etc. Sports: football, swimming, etc.)

Remember

☆ Bit by bit you will start to feel better if you spend time doing things that you love to do.

☆ Create some fun in your life, and you will start to feel a little better.

Chapter 9
Starting Over Again

Where to Turn for Help

In the past few chapters you have heard over and over that it is important to get help while going through all of the ups and downs of the divorce. The next big question is "Where Do I Get Help?"

If Mom and Dad are separated or divorced

and you are hurting a lot inside, you can look for help in many different places. Study the picture below to see some of the people who want to be of help to you.

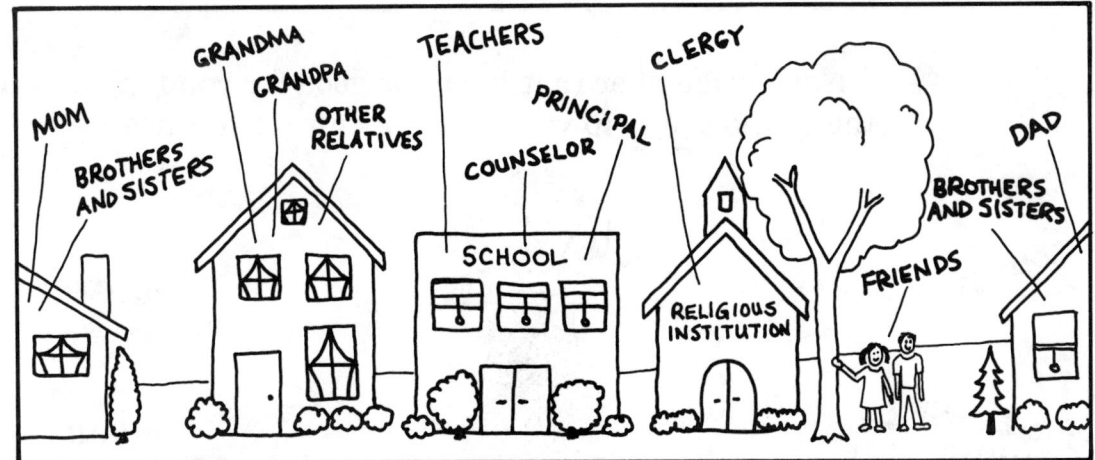

1. Color the picture that shows where you get help when you feel badly about the divorce.

2. Do you have any other places that you can go to for help?

_____
_____

It is important for you to know that there is always someone nearby who can help you with your big problems. Sometimes you need to **reach out** to them and let them know what is going on inside you. Other times people will notice by your words and actions that you are hurting. In that case you need to open yourself to their concern for you.

Take some time to think about one or two things that bother you a lot about the divorce. It could be something about the visitation rules, moving, or money. You may want to look at page 11 where you listed a problem when you started your book many weeks ago. On the lines below, write two of your biggest problems.

Problem #1: _____
_____

Problem #2: _____
_____

Next, remember that it can be good for you to **reach out** to others who can help you through your hard times.

You will find that some people can help you better with some problems and other people can help you better with other problems. Here is a little experiment to help you see how this happens.

"My Who-To-Turn-To Chart"

Put a check in the correct box or write the name of the person who can help you the most with your two problems.

Who Can Help You?	Problem #1	Problem #2
Mom Dad		
Brothers Sisters		
Relatives		
Principal Teachers Counselors		
Doctors Nurses		
Ministers Rabbis Priests		
Others		

Now study your chart. Sometimes only one person can help you while at other times maybe three or four people can support you. The important thing to remember is that

There is always someone nearby to help you!!!

Setting a Goal

Setting goals can be lots of fun.
Setting goals can make you feel like you are very important.
When you set goals, you decide what you *need* in your life,
and how to meet that need.
This can help you feel so good about yourself.

But how do you set goals for yourself? It is easy! You can begin by following three little steps.

☆   1. Decide **what** you need to make yourself feel better.

☆   2. Decide **how much** you need.

☆   3. Decide **when** you need it.

By looking at some samples, you will understand how following these three steps will help you.

My Goal: I want to get rid of my "D" in reading.
- What: I need to raise my reading grade.
- How much: I need to raise it to a "C."
- When: I need to raise it by my next report card.

My Goal: I want to get rid of my fear that nobody in my class likes me.
- What: I need to play with other students in my class.
- How much: I need to ask at least one other student to play with me.
- When: At recess

My Goal: I want to keep in touch with my dad.
- What: I need to keep in contact with my dad.
- How much: I need to see him once a week.
- When: I want to spend one day each weekend with him.

Take some time to think about something in your life that you want to change. By changing it, you will feel much better about yourself. Here are some ideas to get you started.

How to Set a Goal

Every once in awhile, especially when things are looking down for you, you can get the feeling that you are stuck in a rut, that you just do not seem to be able to change anything in your life. This can happen to grown-ups as well as to younger people.

Here are some thoughts that you may have when you are feeling stuck in a rut:

"I'll never have any friends."

"I'm going to fail my math class."

"Daddy will never call me anymore."

"No one ever plays with me."

"My teachers do not like me."

You do not have to sit back and feel like life is controlling you.

Think of being at a really fun sports game. There are two groups of people at the game. One group is on the field calling the plays and making all of the action happen. The other group is sitting on the bench and watching all of the fun and action happen.

Life is like such a game. One group of people takes charge and makes things happen, but another group sits by and watches life happen.

How do you put yourself in charge of your life? It is simple!!! You just need to set some goals for yourself.

Here are some ideas for setting goals:

1. Get up on time.

2. Be on time for school.

3. Eat something for breakfast every day.

4. Get help in school whenever help is needed.

5. Release anger in a healthy way.

6. Tell someone that you need help dealing with the divorce.

Dream some wonderful dreams for yourself.

Think about what you need to make your life a little better.

Then, make it come true by setting your first goal.

My First Goal

What: _____
_____

How much: _____
_____

When: _____
_____

If you live out your goal and it works out well, pat yourself on the back and say "Good Job!" This will lead you to set another goal. Before you know it, you will be feeling really good about yourself.

If your goal does not work out well for you, it does not mean that you are a failure. It simply means that you need to change your goal a little.

Have fun! Set your goals one by one and enjoy feeling good about yourself.

This is a great way to start over!!

A Word Find Review of Key Words from the Divorce Workshop

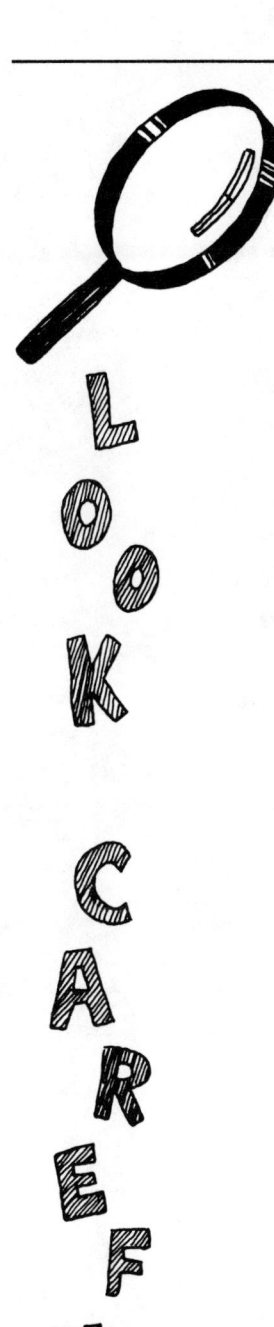

Before you finish your book, take some time to review and search for a few key words.

```
N Z C G H S U X F B C U R M H
O P R M M C S P E C I A L Q L
N Q I H X B V F E K N U D G Y
C U S T O D I A L P A R E N T
U R I H K Z Q H I B M M O I F
S C S D U P S A N D D O W N S
T E H L Q T V S G N E I O K G
O W B Y B O O K S U N R X A Z
D A D F J M P A F J I M E S B
I C G K N P H L O Q A N G E R
A D R U A X P R O B L E M L I
L O S S Z B C T V P I D W F S
P E J N Q G H K O T W R L E C
A C C E P T A N C E H U Z S M
R F S V X B N Y C F L O R T D
E G K P H Q G D I V O R C E M
N U I W A X E A J N E V Z E S
T E A K E T T L E B Y M O M T
```

Divorce   Crisis   Custodial Parent
Mom   Denial   Non-custodial Parent
Dad   Acceptance   Special
Anger   Feelings   Change
Loss   Ups and Downs   Problem
Books   Self Esteem

Certificate of Accomplishment

_____

has worked hard
to complete his/her Loss Journey.

♥

With love and support,
he/she is ready to face the future
and
work through the ups and downs of daily life.

Date _____   Facilitator _____

The Center for Learning

The Center for Learning is a nonprofit corporation founded in 1970 to improve education by developing instructional materials that maximize student involvement. Guided by an ecumenical board of directors, The Center is rooted in values and beliefs reflecting the diversity and unity of our nation. Fellowships, honorariums, donated services, and foundation grants have supported The Center's mission.

The Center for Learning Publications

The Center publishes five series for use in public and private schools. The identifying symbol of a Center for Learning publication is the series registered trademark TAP®—Teachers/Authors/Publishers. Since its inception, The Center has granted several hundred writing fellowships. Working individually or in teams, exceptional teachers from 45 states have created materials that are nationally recognized for their timeliness, endorsement of universal values, and ability to communicate with today's students.

Many effective combinations, depending on student and teacher need, can be selected from approximately 300 titles in the following series: interdisciplinary studies, language arts, novel/drama, religious education, and social studies.

Future Publications

In an effort to keep pace with the changing needs of students and teachers alike, materials are constantly evaluated and updated. Teachers are encouraged to offer suggestions for the development of new publications or revisions of existing titles by writing to The Center for Learning, 21590 Center Ridge Road, Rocky River, Ohio 44116.

The Publishing Team

Rose Schaffer, M.A., Executive Director
Bernadette Vetter, M.A., Associate Director
Diane Podnar, M.S., Production Director
Mary Anne Kovacs, M.A., English Consultant
Lora Murphy, M.A., Social Studies Consultant

Order Information

For a complete listing of titles and price information on books in The Center for Learning series, contact:

The Center for Learning Shipping/Business Office
P.O. Box 910 • Villa Maria, PA 16155
(412) 964-8083 • (800) 767-9090 • FAX (412) 964-8992